SEXY BUT...
True Love Waits

JON BICKNELL

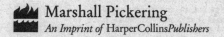
Marshall Pickering
An Imprint of HarperCollinsPublishers

Marshall Pickering is an Imprint of
HarperCollins*Religious*
Part of HarperCollins*Publishers*
77–85 Fulham Palace Road, London W6 8JB
www.christian-publishing.com

First published in Great Britain in 1999
by Marshall Pickering

10 9 8 7 6 5 4 3 2 1

Copyright © 1999 Jon Bicknell

Jon Bicknell asserts the moral right
to be identified as the author of this work

A catalogue record for this book
is available from the British Library

ISBN 0 551 03202 2

Printed and bound in Great Britain by
Caledonian International Book Manufacturing Ltd, Glasgow

CONtENtS

DEDICATION

To Steve Brenkelman, a man I looked up to.
In fact, a man we all looked up to!
The only thing that was too short about
   you was your life.
I miss you.

you often get a response equivalent to 'Yuk!', 'Yum!' or the other one! Some people already know that 'True Love Waits' makes perfect sense; to others it's nonsense, even though they understand what the words mean. To some, maybe even to you, they strike a chord inside somewhere and you just wish that's how it could be. Others like to watch their friends attempt something that they wouldn't dream of doing themselves, even if it's only to see them fail. Whatever the reasons, TLW, like PBJ, always gets a response. Perhaps that's why you bought this book.

The other reason may be the title. Put sex in anything and it sells. For those of you who misread the title, *Sexy But...* is not a book explaining how to get a firmer butt. Sorry about that. But if you're already feeling cheated, you can't sue, because the book does have a bottom line, and the bottom line is this: You are a sexy person! I want you to say those words about yourself out loud right now, wherever you are, and see what happens. If this action gets you detained at Her Majesty's pleasure, remember, my name is Steve Chalke. If, on the other hand, you think you're not a sexy person, then either you're too young really to be reading this, or you're dead. If you fit into any other category at all, you need to say it – now!

Realizing you're a sexy person doesn't mean that you'll end up looking like a Hollywood hunk or babe, however. Chance would be a fine thing! It just means sex is a part of you. Therefore it follows that you probably think about the whole sex thing more often than you're willing to admit to your mother. It means that when you're talking to a mate, and you see someone who looks really fit walk past, as if by magic you totally forget everything you were saying and start uncontrollably dribbling down your chin.

Then, if they unexpectedly smile at you, you end up looking like a rather dodgy mime artist as your arms flap about performing random waving gestures, yet your mouth suddenly becomes the Gobi Desert in a heat wave. Seconds ago the sheet of sandpaper wedged in your mouth passed as a tongue. Now it couldn't form a 'Hi' if you paid it, while your arms continue gyrating like an egg-beater on full power.

It means that despite telling everyone *Baywatch* was 'rubbish', you watched every episode. It means you spend a little too long staring at that perfect stranger you see most days, and almost give the game away that you fancy the pants off them. It means you're normal.

Normal means normal. It's normal to breathe. To eat. To be sexy. No one asks you whether you breathe, they just assume you do. Then there's eaters. No one asks if they eat, they assume they do, so it's then just a matter of what they eat. Of course, a very few can't stomach anything, but most get the salivating munchies at the merest whiff of a bacon sarny (sorry all you vegetarians out there!). I therefore assume that because people are normal, they should be sexy. Sexy is normal. Now here comes the bombshell: God made us sexy. Just like he made us eaty and breathy and sleepy. And before this turns into a rundown of the seven dwarfs (bet you can't name more than six …) I hope you've got my point.

That's why I've called this book *Sexy But … True Love Waits*. It's not the 'Sexy' that's at issue here, but the 'But' – if that's not too confusing! In this book we'll look at what happens when you find yourself turning all sexy, and how a sexy Christian can continue to be one without losing the other. Oh, and we'll talk about the card and why True Love Waits is a Good Thing. However, I don't want you to think that this is a deadly serious text-book approach. No. Instead we'll take a quiet ramble through teenage fumblings together and see if it helps (the ramble, that is, not the fumble). And hopefully by the end we'll see that you can come through the rampant hormone overload you may be feeling at the moment, and survive as a believer.

I thought, however, that I couldn't expect anyone to do something I wouldn't do myself, so self-humiliation starts here. Now I hope you haven't got a clue who I am, but if you have, you'll realize it's impossible to take me too seriously. You'll soon see why! Equally, life has shown me that there's not much point in trying. The racy, laddish magazine *Sky* dubbed me 'The Virginator' and 'The man who wants to stop us having sex before marriage'. When you've read the next chapters you'll see just how ridiculous that sounds! But I'm serious about a lot of things: my faith, my family ... football, of course ... and people like you who are having to make tough choices in amazingly pressurized situations. To me, anyone who can do the right thing then is a hero, no question.

Outside those things, anything else, including my
past, is worth a snigger or two. Let's try not to take
ourselves too seriously. For three decades a famous
lady called Mary Whitehouse was the voice of protest
against explicit language and behaviour on the TV,
and she certainly got people going, either for her
or against her. But perhaps always ranting on about
things isn't the way for committed Christians today.
'Make your point, make a joke and make a friend'
probably works a bit better.

Plenty of earnest Christians may be shocked by
what I'm going to write about in this book. Fortunately
I'm not the first in the queue of those who've publicly
done dumb things. After all, if you read the thick bit of
the Bible, you'll know that a famous Jewish king called
David exposed himself to public ridicule by dancing
well-nigh naked in God's presence. Trouble was, it
wasn't just in God's presence that he did it. No sir!
You could say that if you want to carry on like that,
go ahead, but in the privacy of your own palace.
However, he exposed a lot more of himself to public
ridicule than normally meets the eye! His wife Michal
(yes, that is a woman's name) obviously lacked

nothing in the looks department, but did in the one marked 'sense of humour'. Anyway, she blew a fuse at this. If she'd had more sense, she shouldn't have got crazy; she should have sold tickets!

Matt Redman wrote a popular worship song quoting the words David spoke about that famous session in 2 Samuel 6:22: 'I will become even more undignified than this, and I will be humiliated in my own eyes.' So if you ask me why I'm writing this, I'll say that I'm merely taking my cue from there. That's why this book may be a bit different from other Christian books on sex that you've seen, because the 'Sexy But' bit is more 'hands on' (in a manner of speaking) than them. There are some really great books for Christians, but talking and writing about something personal like sex isn't just about bringing in all the theoretical ideas, as you probably know yourself.

It seems everybody today likes to get inside the real-life, embarrassing stuff to do with other people's intimate bits. If you disagree, you haven't seen the average teenager turn straight to the problem pages of the magazines they read. It's not just because it's a laugh, it's because we'd like to believe that those letters are true (though sometimes you can hardly believe it!) and that we're not unique when things go pear-shaped for us. That's why I decided to 'get it all out in the open', because it happened. All I can hope for is that it doesn't put you off your dinner!

Fortunately for me, I've never questioned my orientation (if you don't know what that is, it's got nothing to do with running through woods holding a compass) because, apart from an innocent incident of mutual bottom examination at the age of 10 in a tree-house with a boy called Bruno, I never doubted that I always fancied girls. (Well, at that age, stuck up in a tree all day, you just run out of things to compare ...) What I always doubted was that they would fancy me back.

So I hope you'll understand that talking about sex is often not straightforward, because you're really talking about people, and most people are a complex mix of things, not all of which they have full control of. Equally, because you can't cut the sex bit out of what makes a person who they are, you can end up with a naff self-image because you've tried all sorts of self-deluded and stupid things to try to rectify that. Before

I became a Christian my self-image was total pants, and I thank God that he knocked on the door of my heart when I was 16, and did a rescue job before I had a chance to make it any worse.

That one event, becoming a Christian, changed everything. I knew afterwards that I could look at myself differently, that I could value myself. Suddenly I realized I had great value in God's eyes, because Jesus paid a flippin' big price to show it – in other words he gave his life up for me. That's got to mean that he thinks I'm important. Therefore I can write what I've written because I'm not out to make myself feel important, neither am I out to shock deliberately. I'm not searching for anyone else's approval, because I don't need it, and I sleep soundly at night knowing I'm loved.

Not that I feel smugly self-satisfied, but it's just so good to come through the traumas that you'll read about in a little while, and realize that an insignificant bloke like me still matters to the Creator of the Universe. That's why I've chosen to recall these events, so that if something like this is happening, or has happened, to you, you'll begin to see that it's not the end of the world. I hope this book will help you to sense how valu-able you are too.

To put it as simply as possible, all the important details about the message of True Love Waits really stem from that message. If you don't know you're loved, then you won't be able to put a true value on stuff. It would be a bit like going abroad and not knowing the right exchange rate for your money. You'd simply end up taking less than its true worth for everything you get. The only answer is to say, 'No. I know what the true value is. I know the value of my body, my purity, even my life. So stop trying to con me!'

1

GiNgeR nUts aNd
OTHER BISCUITS

God likes a laugh. No doubt about it. If you're a bloke like me and you've got ginger hair – the joke's on you. We can almost hear him chuckling away to himself. Ha ha. Very funny. Good joke – not! He didn't need to bother creating us, but he was obviously bored one day, and the thought of endlessly looking down from above on brown, black and blonde barnets made him think, 'What the heck, variety is the spice of life. After all, the angels could do with a laugh, they've been

looking so solemn recently. This'll get them giggling –
I'll sprinkle a few redheads about...' And, as I believe
it might say somewhere in the Bible (perhaps), 'So it
came to pass that on the sixth day the Lord God said:
"Gabriel, take a butcher's at those tangerine tops,
verily verily, don't they look bonkers..." '

Of course, there is an alternative way of looking at
how gingers came to pass. If you don't think it was
God's fault, you can blame the Fall. The Fall occurred
when Adam and Eve decided that a state of eternal
paradise wasn't as useful as being able to choose
your own fruit salad, and mankind as a whole suffered
the consequences of this one rather rash act. Now, all
I'm saying on the matter is that it would have been
nice if Adam had consulted us first, because if Adam
was to blame for my carrot-coloured head carpet,
then I'll be making a bee-line for the little Figgy fellow
once I'm inside the Pearly Gates. I'll know which one
he is, because he'll be the only one without a tummy
button (think about it). I for one will most definitely be
'having a word', as they say on *Eastenders*.

If my hair colouring was never God's idea, but
was one of those awful consequences of man's sin,

and it can be put down fairly and squarely to Mr and Mrs Adam, then I'm choked. I suppose that would put us into the same 'Post-Fall' bucket as other pointless things. Like stinging nettles.

If the *Sun* newspaper had been around at the time, the headlines would have read: 'Out – Mankind! In – Nettles and Ginger Spice!' Trouble is, stingers seem to have a whole lot better time of it than gingers. Take stinging for example. Picture Adam out one day picking flowers for his missus. He spies a new green plant growing around his allotment and thinks, 'A lovely new plant to go in my wife's displays. I'll call it "Nettle" and take some back for her ... Ouch!' You quickly see how it got its name. People have learnt not to mess. But back to gingers. What this little meander down the garden path goes to prove is that gingers can't escape the fact – we're definitely scraping the bottom of the 'Post-Fall' barrel.

However, after quite a few thousands of years, even God has recently started to warm towards us. Ginger hair has been increasingly 'on the up' for a while now. God obviously thinks we deserve a break. Talking of breaks, I think it all started with snooker star Steve

Davis. He was the first. Boring maybe, but God had to start somewhere. Then it was Mick Hucknell of Simply Red. Mick relied on his amazing voice to project the band to stardom, and only then did he whip his flat cap off to reveal that underneath it all lay a dread-locked ginger bonce of awesome proportions. Then, of course, we have to thank our own patron saint, the gigantic and thoroughly ginger Chris Evans. Equally, we can't forget various scampering Manchester United football stars. If you think one or two of them have hair which clashes with their scarlet tops, relax. It's not your TV on the blink. Their god-like gift on the ball just about defies their ghastly God-gift on the barnet.

Yet when I was growing up, it was quite different. Not even a hint of gingerness anywhere, apart from ... er ... guinea pigs. Back then, the only successful ginger-haired role model we had was the school guinea pig. Naturally, such a thing may easily start to unhinge a young, fresh-faced lad like myself. I had to choose between imitating a life spent nibbling sec-ondhand lettuce leaves, or I had to go it alone.

Going it alone has its own drawbacks, however. You realize very soon that several career options are simply not going to come through for gingers. Take crime for instance. As an angry 15-year-old I contemplated a life of thievery. My initial enthusiasm was dulled considerably when I thought about being caught, and the inevitable identity parade. How exactly do you try to hide this hair? 'Easy,' I hear you say, 'shave it off!'

Sounds easy, right? Wrong! Let me tell you about the late 1970s and men's hair. There were two sacred rules set in stone about hair back then: (1) Big; (2) Permy. The bigger, the permier, the better. To give you an example, the initials on the BP petrol stations don't stand for anything sensible like British Petroleum. No, BP stands for Big Perm, and because that was 'the Look', everybody started buying their petrol there. Sounds reasonable, doesn't it? In the 1970s afros the size of the Hindenburg airship floated gracefully over the top of blokes' skulls, defying gravity, low ceilings and strong winds. Those were the days when cars had vinyl roofs and men had hair which you could lose a small dog in. It was just how things were.

The only exception to this was Errol Brown, the lead singer with Hot Chocolate, who was brown, sexy and very bald, and made up for it with a hugely suggestive moustache. For a lad like me, however, baldness outside a mental institution was not an option. 'OK,' I hear you answer, 'if you won't shave it off, why don't you change its colour?' Well yes, the strange and wonderful world of hair dye was beckoning by then, but it wasn't that simple. At that time hair dyeing was a science producing such dubious results that it felt as if you were entering a twilight world of hocus pocus from which you might never emerge again. But it was worth a go, wasn't it?

Actually no. If you think that God would let his finest practical joke be scuppered by a £2.50 jar of hair dye, I suggest that you underestimate the clever old sausage. Anyone tempted to do this with ginger hair will find that God thought about this possibility long before the idea ever crossed your mind. And he built in a nasty little booby trap. If you try to dye it, ginger hair won't hold up a white flag and surrender. Instead it goes a bright colour far removed from what you had in mind. Isn't God clever? Humorous, too. *Very* funny. When you try to dye ginger hair brown, it comes out green – yes, a very bright, vivid green at that.

Not that I've ever tried it with my own hair. Oh no. I didn't wish to enter the 'twilight zone' with my hair. I did dip my toe in the waters, though. Or rather, to be factually accurate, I dipped my eyebrows in. I tried to dye them brown. They turned Dipsy Teletubby green.

Getting back to thievery, even my fertile imagination couldn't see a future for a daring, infamous cat-burglar carrying off bags of jewel-laden swag, leaving a description for any witness within 50 yards: 'Oh yes, I'd recognize him again, he's the one with green eyebrows.' I think you'd agree it would make slipping anonymously into a crowd slightly more tricky... Eventually I did recover my original eyebrow colouring, after numerous washes with Vanish, but it showed me that I was hopelessly lumbered with my lot, and like Adam with those nettles I'd learnt not to mess. The hair on top of my head was there to stay, while my fledgling life of crime would sadly have to go. To misquote the old prison motto: 'If you can't do the time ... don't dye the barnet.'

No, it became very clear why snooker star Steve Davis was forced to retreat to his snooker table for hours and hours of lonely practice, and Chris Evans to the sanctuary of the anonymous radio microphone in his room. It's just not fair. No teenager wants to stand out like a sore thumb, or, for that matter, a sore any other bit. Most teenagers, myself included, just want to be liked by everybody else; no more, no less. God wasn't through with me, however. He had no intention of making me just like everybody else. His chuckle-a-gram had only just started, and because this is actually a book about sex, and not just about ginger hair, this is where we get personal.

It's like this: if I was going to have ginger hair, I was also going to have ginger hairs. By the age of 12 I'd realized that God's masterplan for gingers didn't just stop at the top. Oh no. In fact, when this finally dawned on me, I decided that it was really quite a sick joke. It appeared that God intended me to have ginger body hair as well. On my legs, my arms, my chest (some hopes), under my arms and finally, and most unpleasantly, under my pants. Yes, God had decided to go for the all-in-one look. A bit like my Dad used to do with magnolia paint when he was redecorating.

Why it had to be this way I still can't fathom. He hasn't always been mean with his colours (God, that is, not my Dad). Take peacocks, for example. The bloke peacocks were given an amazing variety of colours in their tail plumage alone, whereas gingers come away with a bargain-basement, all-in, job-lot special (even in the peacock department, if that's not being too rude)!

It started to get worse, a lot worse, as my first delivery of this job lot failed to turn up. I waited and waited. I became increasingly impatient for any sort of curly ginger fellows to put in an appearance. They seemed to have missed the hormone bus and instead decided to walk. A very long, meandering, 'it doesn't matter what time we get there' walk.

Thirteenth birthday; no pubic hair. The pubic hair fairy didn't leave a happy little bundle underneath my pillow, or more importantly, underneath my armpits. Fourteenth birthday; same story. I was beginning to draw up contingency plans, as it appeared alarmingly that even the pubic hair stork couldn't be bothered to flap by. Now I was the one getting in a flap, a big flap. It was a joke, and it was all on me. Or rather it wasn't. Not even one curly little chap anywhere, and believe me I searched. Boy, did I search. I think I nearly went half-blind in the process, yet to no avail. There was nothing for it, this was a total and utter emergency – I would have to get the crayons out.

My first experiment with crayons wasn't good. You just couldn't press hard enough to get enough colour down and boy, did it hurt. I was also a bit anxious about lead poisoning in my private parts. When blokes crudely talked about having 'lead in your pencil' they usually meant that you'd got a girl pregnant. At the rate I was going, I imagined that in my case it might end up being taken literally. It was desperate stuff anyway, and it wasn't working. Crayons inevitably gave way to felt-tips.

With felt-tips the problem of colour density was solved to a certain extent, but not without a price. My worst nightmare was of standing in the school show-ers after games and having browny-red streaks run-ning down the insides of my legs as the felt-tip ran! I imagined being carted off to a loony bin for 'tests' after being exposed by our psychopathic games teacher in the shower wearing nothing but smudged, felt-tip pubic hairs! Still, I suppose then I would have ended up in a sanatorium with my head shaved. As they say, every cloud does have its silver lining...

Back to reality. While other lads in my year at school were having to harvest their own body hair for fear of turning into Esau's double (a hairy biblical bloke, if you don't know), I would gladly have purchased their pubic off-cuts and stuck them on in various strategic positions if the colour match was anywhere near possible. The school psychopath insisted on 'shower hell', and I trailed nakedly in the wake of these boys with hairy underarms and even hairier undercarriages. One lad called Stephen Mockett was so hairy, he could give an entire pencil shop a run for its money. I cringed. Mocked by Mockett. This period was, in the words of Winston Churchill, 'my darkest hour'. 'Never, in the history of puberty, has so much been grown by so many, compared to so few.'

Death or body hair had to arrive soon. By then I honestly didn't care which. Fortunately the latter popped out one day when I popped out to the shops. Later, when I found it on my daily Baldness Inspection, I thought perhaps it was a stray one from my head that had flown south for the winter, but there it was. Unquestionably. The real thing. But could it stand the acid test?

I pulled at it tentatively, and felt an almost giddy sense of elation as my new-found friend stuck fast. Immediately I wanted to ring up the famous children's television programme of the time, *John Craven's Newsround*, with what would undoubtedly be the main news item on that day's round-up. I even thought of sending the particular hair off, except that it was more of a rare and endangered species than all of those white rhinos that John Craven was always harping on about. Amazingly though, more followed. Not white rhinos that is, but body hairs. Like a dairy farmer with a small herd, I started to name each one. I was among friends. They were few; but they were loved and they were mine, no matter how infuriatingly curly they were.

I had truly turned a corner. Suddenly I now felt that I could potentially achieve something sexually with a girl. It wasn't that I had any particular girl in mind for this – I was far too 'nice' for such a thing – it was just that biologically there was now a slim chance that I could get a girl pregnant, according to what I recalled from Biology lessons about lactating mammals and Sammy Sperm. I started walking down the corridor with a stupid grin on my face at such thoughts, though what I had to be proud of, heaven only knows. Fortunately, unlike the lesser spotted toads we studied in Biology, the opposite sex weren't permanently gagging for it. In fact, with that stupid grin on my face they most certainly would have gagged on the very thought of it. Yes, if I'd even mentioned it to a girl I'm sure she would have been physically sick on the spot. Oh well, you've got to start somewhere.

Unfortunately, my tale of woe doesn't end there. No. That wasn't the end of my Hammer House of Hairless Horrors. Squeamish boys and parents may want to jump on a few pages. God had a ghastly last laugh in store. This is sex education at its most graphic and eye watering. So here goes. Every bloke has one, therefore let's talk willies...

2

OUCh!

Fat little cherubs, butt-naked and shooting water out of their willies. If you've ever been on a French exchange trip and looked around any dodgy old chateaux, you'll know what I'm talking about. If I was a French Marquis (that's not a big tent for wedding receptions) from the sixteenth century or whenever, I'm sure I could think of better ways of spending lorry-loads of filthy francs than buying fountains full of these little fat fellows. And 'little' is the operative word. Their willies are tiny!

I doubt this was just to save materials, because the sculptors who made them always seemed to give them podgy little bellies, so it can't have been that. Perhaps they didn't want to arouse sensitive young female members of the French aristocracy unwittingly with more attention-grabbing willies. Whatever the reason, next time you get within eyeshot of one, stare at their irrigation tackle for a while longer than is good for you, and notice something else.

Let's call it 'the business end'. How exactly do you try and describe it? Well, perhaps the business end could be compared to the top of a very small velvet purse, neatly pulled together with a drawstring (though obviously without the drawstring attached). That extra bit left over is modelled on the real thing, and is the top of the foreskin. On the real article, it cleverly acts like the dustcap on the valve bit of a car tyre. This can be undone and taken off. If you have a very young brother, please don't take the dustcap comparison too far – in fact, no matter how curious you are, don't try to unscrew and throw away his endy-bit! Willies don't work that way. Intense pain is likely to ensue. Which brings me onto the subject of this chapter.

As a nation, the Jews got it right with their policy towards baby boys. At eight days – that's it. They perform a symbolic ritual on the unsuspecting boy which has been nicknamed 'The Unkindest Cut of All'. Those little foreskins are ceremonially snipped away without so much as a by-your-leave, and from that day onwards another little Jewish boy's eyes will unwittingly water whenever sharp knives and synagogues are mentioned in the same sentence. Apparently it's generally believed to be better for you and much more hygienic, particularly in a hot climate. After the operation the willy still does every-thing it was intended to do without any harm, but by the time you're old enough to digest such handy medical facts, you don't feel like volunteering to have it done!

Girls, it's not like giving blood – not even if you go private! To give you some idea of the pain involved, in Genesis 34 Jacob's sons trick some gullible blokes into being circumcised. The blokes agree, thinking they might then get a chance with the ladies. In verse 25 we read: 'Three days later, while all of them were still in pain...' Jacob's brothers then double-crossed them, chopping off more than just a bit of skin. In fact, they did them in. Nice!

Next time you're watching *Match of the Day* and you witness a professional footballer under the full glare of dozens of cameras taking a nasty belter you know where, you'll also know that for the following minute he's completely helpless. John 'Motty' Motson has to say something to snigger at to fill the time, because the player can't just get up and 'run it off' – despite the fact that 30,000 spectators, his entire family and several million viewers are waiting for him to get over it and rejoin the game. That particular pain barrier definitely can't be overcome by mind over matter.

Anyway, to go back to the average Western willy, you'll find they're quite a clever piece of engineering. Those blokes who have passed painlessly through puberty will know that as your willy gets bigger, so the foreskin naturally finds its own place, often just below the head of the penis. So let's return to this semi-hairy 15-year-old. While other lads took their opportunity to display their new extra inches in the school showers, I realized that all the boys who strutted about showing off (I swear some of those lads thought they were at the Horse of the Year Show) had willies where the foreskin obliged – but not mine.

As my own equipment attempted to take up the challenge, I'd gained a commendable few inches (thanks be to God), yet this minor matter of the fore-skin remained. It simply refused to do the business. It wasn't going anywhere. It just sat there – cherub-like. This wasn't going to make me a sex-god, or a sex-anything for that matter. So I thought I'd better give it a helping hand. This proved to be a very enjoyable experience.

Boys have always fiddled. Some will carry on fid-dling till the cows come home. Morning, noon and night, some can't stop themselves. Alternatively, a few sensitive lads feel hideously guilty at the slightest fumble, or more than 'two shakes' in the urinals. But the fascination, and the pleasure of having a tank with a 'w', remains. It's not actually helped by the fact that most lads of that age can have a passable erection just by thumbing through the fashion sections of their granny's clothes catalogue. And that features 30-something models in tight-fitting tops and sensible slacks, let alone what happens when you get to the bra and panties section...

Then there are ripped-out bits of porno magazines purchased by the big lads at school, which get passed around in smaller and smaller bits to satisfy a hungry market. On top of that you get the stories from such magazines. Most make your eyes bulge, let alone anything else! Then there's been the recent rise in slightly more subtle magazines, which are still basically intended to give a rise of another sort. All of these are the staple diet of bloke masturbators the world over.

Me, I was doing OK, keeping my end up – as they say. And actually, if you're a Christian, nowhere in the Bible is it frowned upon. However, back to the foreskin. The stupid thing wouldn't stay where it was supposed to. So one day while I was in the bath (it's amazing how many baths lads of that age suddenly need to take...) I thought, 'Right, I'll force the issue. This time it's going to do what I say. This time it's going to stay.' Sure enough, it did, but as my enthusiasm for what I'd just achieved passed, I realized the pain hadn't. Somehow, I think mother nature didn't intend this, and now she was going to show me who was boss. Despite my best efforts, I couldn't return the offending foreskin to its previous place. Like a woman with fat hands trying to get a ring off, the more I tried, the redder and sorer the thing got. I sheepishly retired to bed hoping that the morning would bring some relief.

Instead the morning brought more pain. The instant I woke up, I knew all was not well. As I tentatively looked down at the scene of the crime, I was worryingly aware of what was causing the throbbing. If you've ever tightened an elastic band around your finger, you'll know that not only does the end of your finger go red, it also swells up. *Touché*. It was all getting horribly out of hand 'downstairs'. I went off to school in a fog of fear. Was the end of my willy just going to drop off in my pants sometime during the day, as was the fate of newly-born boy lambs who had a similar thing done to them by the vet? I waited with baited breath.

The sensible and level-headed among you will say at this point, 'Why didn't you just go to a doctor?' Well, looking back, that would have been infinitely better than what was to come. However, what was to come came. My Dad, who knew nothing about this self-inflicted punishment, decided that just he and I should visit my grandparents together for the weekend. He saw this as a bonding thing. To me I couldn't see beyond the very burning thing that I was feeling. The pain continued to grip my genitals in its vice-like hold. Yet I managed somehow to make it through the whole of that weekend until we got home on the Sunday. By then I'd reached a state of near-delirium with the pain, and had to tell my Dad. This also involved showing him. He was horrified. This worried me even more as, unlike me, it wasn't physically attached to him.

The next morning, little did the staff of my local health centre know, but that day was going to see them standing around and gawping open-mouthed at 'The Incredible Inflating Willy'. To be fair, they were very sympathetic. But what they insisted on doing was definitely not. They took a bowl of freezing water with ice in it, held it just below my willy, and plunged it in for what seemed like hours at a time. Up to that point, it felt like my willy was reaching nuclear meltdown temperatures, but now, by hideous contrast, this vile torture followed. Just when I thought I was going to get some partial relief, they took it out, but only to try and force the angry skin back into place. The Russian KGB couldn't have imagined a worse combination of humiliation and torture if they'd tried. It was all, however, to no avail.

So off to hospital I went. The nurse who admitted me before the operation was cheerful and good natured, but when 10 minutes later she returned with a razor and said that it was 'time for my shave', it wasn't my chin that she was eyeing up! She happily informed me that I would have to be completely shaved for the operation. Of course my heart sank. 'My friends!' I thought to myself. What was going to happen to my little pubic posse? This was obviously no problem for her, she just shaved them all away without so much as a second thought for my babies. In fact, her only comment to me throughout this whole hideous scene was, 'You haven't got many hairs, have you?' To her this was just trying to be chatty. To me it was the cold, callous voice of a murderer. I completely hated her!

So here I was again, back to Square One on the pubic scale, and just about to have a bit of my willy chopped off. Things were not looking good.

After the operation, I didn't wish to look at how things were. Slowly the pain died down, but the huge bandages gave testimony to surgery of a worryingly serious kind. Shoals of trainee doctors came round and stood with clipboards and alarmed expressions, staring at my genitals. Well actually, it was the male doctors who were alarmed. The female ones were trying not to giggle. I was depressed. My family came by during visiting hours. I was deeply depressed.

What can you say to an acutely embarrassed 15-year-old who has lost bits off his willy, and all his pubic hair to boot – 'How are you?' They told me it could have been worse. I couldn't imagine anything worse, until the elderly patient in the next bed kept screaming out in the middle of the night, 'It's gone! It's gone! Where's it gone?' and I knew he wasn't just talking about his copy of the *Daily Mirror*. Yes, it was gone, and yes, they'd taken it. In fact, because of cancer, they'd sawn it clean off. Ouch!

If you've read this far, congratulations. If you like happy endings, I'm delighted to tell you that basically they performed a bit of a tricky circumcision. Everything is now in perfect order, and I have two children to prove it. Joanna, my wife (yes, more on her later), says it's just how she would have wanted it anyway, so that's all right then...

3

FrEe wilLy

The introduction to this book talks about being sexy. Even after all that had happened, those feelings still survived in me. Equally, whatever you go through, they'll remain in you too and surface at some stage, perhaps when you're least expecting them. What also happened for me a bit later on was that I became a Christian. And like most Christian teenagers, I became rather interested in what God might have to say on the subject of sex.

St Paul wrote much of the New Testament, and it contains a lot of good stuff. It's not all theory to do with life after death, however. Most Christians alive today are also quite keen on life *before* death. So were the Christians to whom Paul wrote. In fact, there was an openly randy bunch of Christians in Corinth who got more than their fair share – and they got lots of letters too! Sorry if that idea upsets you, but if they hadn't been so randy we'd never have got so much of 1 and 2 Corinthians, and we'd have been the losers.

Paul was never one to go on like this: 'Thus says the Lord – lads, you need to run away from women and hide yourselves in a monastery if you want to be good Christians.' No. Rather his sentiment was something like this: 'Face up to yourselves. Of course you have these feelings, but don't feed your sexual appetite if it's damaging your faith.'

This may come as a shock to those of you who are praying like mad that your sexual desires would just go away, and saying that you'd become a totally different person without any of those troublesome temptations. Rather than praying that your sexual desires would go away, I believe that through prayer you receive power to go away from your dodgy sexual desires. Do you get it? *You* go away, rather than they go away. Either way, with Jesus in there with you, they can get sorted. As Paul said, 'God did not give us a spirit of timidity, but a spirit of power, of love and of self-discipline' (2 Timothy 1:7).

To put it another way, the Captain of the *Titanic* could have prayed that God would just remove the iceberg from the sea, while still steaming full speed ahead, or he could simply have used the power of the engines to steer the ship away from the iceberg before it was too late. (When it came to the crunch, of course, that particular bloke did neither...)

When you start to think like this, you realize that all sorts of problems you're struggling with are not necessarily going to evaporate into thin air. The answer to prayer you imagine you'll get may not be the one that actually arrives.

In reality, the one where everything becomes miraculously easy is quite rare, because God's answer may be the one where you become stronger in the situation, while the situation itself remains disarmingly unchanged. St Paul had to learn this lesson too, and God had to remind him, 'My power is at its best in weakness' (2 Corinthians 12:9). That way it's not going to kill you to live with these things. Now you may agree with this in theory, but also answer that it's not quite that simple in reality. OK then, let's face reality, right here and right now.

Take blokes and their erections, for example. I'm not going to beat about the bush on this one (no smutty jokes, please!) because if you're a bloke, and you're a teenager, you're going to have loads of these – that's erections, not smutty jokes … Indeed, it's a hard fact of life that when you're a bloke of that age, that's quite often what it is – hard. So fellas, praying for your erection to go away while watching a very sexy film is not as helpful as turning over to *News at Ten*. If it still continues throughout the rest of the news, then I really suggest you consult a doctor!

Not that the ability to get an erection at awkward moments goes away as you get older. In fact, nothing much changes for the next 20 to 40 years, so firstly you don't have to be alarmed by all those sexual articles that say your libido – the amount of sexual energy you have – dramatically trails off after the age of 19. Such comments are designed to make you afraid, and who gains most when Christians worry and fret unnecessarily? Exactly. Whoever it is, it's not Jesus, that's for sure. That thinking opens the door to those demonic little voices that get on your shoulder and whisper, 'Go on, get in there my son, before it's too late...' Before you fall for that lie, think about the expression 'dirty old man', and let me appeal to your logical mind for a minute.

Why do you think people are called 'dirty old men'? Simple: because they haven't been reading the same articles that got you so stressed. Their own bodies, far from giving them the message that their sexual drive should have tailed off dramatically, are telling them something else. Basically, dirty old men are still getting signals from their bodies telling them that they're 19 years old. And they're stupid enough, or reckless enough, to believe them.

Of course, if sex experts say your sexual drive (or libido) tails off, then I'm not going to argue, but it's a bit like saying Manchester United's attendances are falling because they're only getting 54,000 compared to 57,000. You get my point? That's still an awful lot of people, and there's probably still an awful lot of sex waiting ahead of you even if you wait until you're in later life before you start. You see, fellas, that sexual drive of yours won't need re-tarmacking for a very long time...

Therefore, don't think that every erection you have will somehow mean you've got less deposits in the bank for later. Amazingly, the way God made this ingenious thing to work means it can go up and down, and up and down, with monotonous regularity, or exciting predictability, depending on how you choose to look at it. So you don't need to be swept into believing you must have sex now because the desire will go if you wait a few more years. That's rubbish!

And by the way, talking of looking at it, and not that I've done much research on the subject, apparently the vast majority of willies are all more or less similar in length when they're hard (about 6 inches or 150 millimetres). There are exceptions, just like there are people who take size 14 trainers, but their number is dwarfed by the number of wishful-thinking boasters out there!

Apparently, however, there are big differences when willies are limp (or, to use the hideous technical term, 'flaccid'). Then they can range from tiny to huge, right up to 'The Lunchbox' from *The Full Monty*! And you can't tell by looking at the bloke how big it's likely to be. Big hands, big feet or big noses don't automatically mean big willies – especially if it's in the middle of winter! After all, it's not just brown bears that can hibernate – and have you seen some of those incredibly muscly body-builder types? It's not just their posing pouches that are miniscule – the contents seem to have undergone some kind of Japanese bonsai tree makeover!

While we're on the subject of size, it's a fact that far more people than you imagine wonder at some stage whether they're big enough to 'get the job done', and later whether their sperm count (by the way, that's not basic maths classes for the little chaps!) is going to be good enough. Some of you may be sitting there with confident smiles on your faces, thinking 'I've got no problems, pal!' For others among you, you may even now be spending fretful hours on this very thought. I don't wish to underestimate the amount of stress that this worry causes, but it's actually all part of growing up, as much part of growing up for a bloke as learning to programme a video player...

The problem here is partly caused by those same glossy, blokeish magazines that I mentioned earlier, which always feature a lust-hungry babe on the front cover just starting to emerge from her tantalizing attire. These aren't necessarily pornographic mags, but the ones that people like W.H. Smith's sell under the title of 'lifestyle' magazines. They're still a bit dodgy all the same, because you quite often get tales about amazing sexual gymnastics, or about some 'lucky' punter with a 10-inch todger who can keep it up all night, then step straight into his Armani suit for a thrusting day at the office. Basically, in all these mags, bigger is always better, whether it's a motor, a holiday, or a knob. And sorry, but you may well be one if you're taken in by it.

Actually I believe that our sulphurous enemy stands behind it all, and smiles as yet another relatively well-balanced bloke starts feeling inadequate at the thought of what he's not. If you don't believe me, try this little test. Imagine one such magazine.

Imagine the babe on the front. Imagine staring into those sultry eyes (the *eyes*, I said!) as she stands in front of you. You are you. I assume you don't drive a Lamborghini, live in Monte Carlo, or holiday on Mustique. (Maybe a Metro, Staines and Minehead, right?) The question is, how are you going to get her to fall in love with you?

You'll soon realize how easy it is for normal, well-balanced blokes to feel intimidated, because you *are* just normal and not a superstar superstud. But remember, it's a game. Magazine life isn't real life. Sure, there are some women out there for whom big and bulging may be the only words that matter, but if I were you, don't fall for the impression that anything less is less. It's not.

Having said that, however, all blokes would like to think that they're something exceptional, so you can understand why such magazines sell so well. Secretly, we'd all like to know that someone adores us for what we are, and I suppose until Jesus returns, this need to bolster fragile male egos is one of the most basic needs of humanity. All I can say is, I hope he's on his way soon...

4

FrEe wiLLy 2

Until Jesus returns, we have the body we've got and for the lads, a willy comes as standard. It's brilliantly made, but it has one crucial design flaw. It has no brains whatsoever. Not that God made a boo-boo on this one, because he made up for the lack by giving you brains, not between your legs, but between your ears. However, your brain's design flaw is that it's positioned approximately three feet from the action.

This means in practice that your brain can be persuaded it has nothing to do with that department, when it was very much intended to be involved with what goes on down there! Herein lies the problem. The number of lads who shortcut the process and 'think with their dicks' is legion, simply because they can't be bothered to think with the real thing. Probably this is because it might not give them the answers they want to hear. However, thinking with your dick doesn't really happen either. A lot may happen with them, but thinking isn't part of it...

Let's suppose you do think with your head when you're around the opposite sex. Good for you. But you'll know yourself that it just gets an awful lot harder if your head is stuffed full of sexy images acquired along the way from videos and mags. Of course we all enjoy looking at well-taken photos of gorgeous people, but too much means you're never far from the ideas they create.

Don't get me wrong, they look fantastic – that's not in dispute. What is in dispute is whether you're able to keep thinking straight if you treasure these pictures, say by smothering your bedroom walls with them.

When you close your eyes at night, they're there, and when you open them in the morning, they're still there. Having sexy images on your walls is no crime, neither is having them in your head, but it does cause a problem to lots of people, especially believers.

Believers can have sexy thoughts that they're careful with, or they can have ones that run all over the place like demented little fluffy animals let out of cages. The choice is yours. If your thoughts are running all over the place, you can spend so much time trying to round them up that in the end you just capitulate and say, 'To hell with it, just do what comes naturally.' It's because the alternative takes more effort to get sorted.

So how do you start to sort it? Firstly, recognize who the Boss is. If it's Jesus, or that's who you want to be the Boss, then it's a great place to start. Now you have to decide. You can let your brains tell you what to do, responding to your heart, or you can let your willy tell you what to do. If you've decided to 'do the right thing', your heart will always come into it, and will be pushing you to walk close to Jesus. Then it's two against one. No matter how insistent your willy gets, it

You may say that sounds much too deep, and going out is just about having a laugh and belonging together, and shouldn't be made to sound so complicated. Well, yes and no. Going out with someone you love is great. It's one of the best of human experiences, but throughout the time you're going out, the reality is that the blokes will have to decide who's calling the shots – their heads, their hearts, or their willies. This is probably going to happen regardless of whether he's a Christian, or she's a Christian, and even whether you lead a Christian group together.

Now lads, if you're going out with someone, and you're aware of this sort of problem, and you feel that your willy is in danger of behaving much too friskily for your own liking, fear not! We've compiled a few ways of showing it who's Boss. A small team of experts (i.e. me and my mate Dave) have been assembled to offer you the most comprehensive guide to hiding any possible trouser problems. This advice is compiled not to focus on the subject of erections, but because you're probably serious about living as a Spirit-led Christian. Yet you also have the tension of living with feeling sexy. Equally, if you're going out with a girl you want to impress, impress her in a way that you'll still feel proud of later.

So if you're a bloke, and you don't want to fall foul of the old 'Is that a gun in your pocket, or are you just pleased to see me?' line, then it's best that you follow carefully...

Firstly, however, a warning. There's no hard and fast rule as to when a bloke will have a hard-on. Everyone says that blokes are more likely than girls to be turned on by something they see, a person they can watch, or a picture they can ogle over. Others remain unmoved until things start getting 'touchy-feely'. Either way, girls and blokes are definitely different.

To give you an example, take the school dinner queue. While some of the girls may be feeling sick at the smell of acres of boiled cabbage, some of the blokes who are pressed up against someone fanciable may be feeling something, but it won't be sick, and it definitely won't have anything to do with cabbage. Don't be alarmed, girls: not every bloke out there is waiting for bangers and mash with a smutty smirk on his face, but I'm just letting you know!

Unfortunately, some Christian books merely give advice telling girls to dress less provocatively, but as you can see, it also often depends on the number of sexual images already zinging around in there. The trouble is, you can't tell which bloke will react which way just by looking at them, because it's not actually your fault what happens inside a bloke's mind. The bloke has to be responsible for his own thoughts, and his own tackle, despite what you look like. This works the other way too, lads. If you deliberately flirt in a way that's a calculated come-on but which you have no intention of being responsible for, then grow up!

Finally, lads, remember that the very same healthy sexuality that you're struggling to manage right now is the one which will come in so handy later on. You may end up choosing this particular girl to be your wife, but more likely not, so don't make a fool of yourself, or your faith, at this stage. If you're still a virgin, be proud of the fact. You haven't sold yourself short, and by God's grace you never will.

Actually having the sex that he's dreaming of doesn't make that much difference. It doesn't all get sorted just because you slept with the object of your desire. If it did, the people having uncommitted sex right now wouldn't two-time, or find themselves fantasizing about someone else. Having sex doesn't cure anything, and most people's experience will tell you that instead it just makes things very much more complicated!

You, however, are different. All the while you're gaining a powerful self-control, the final fruit of the Spirit, that will take you through times when you'll need it in future life, whether you get married or not.

One of the best reasons for waiting is that you learn to work out your differences and disagreements with your partner by communication. Having sex with someone in the early part of a relationship just papers over the inevitable differences you have. This may be OK for those one-dimensional people who only want a very superficial relationship, but if you both want to be committed to each other it will never do. It's like smashing the window of your car because you want a bit of fresh air – you get your fresh air, but at what price, and why couldn't you wait to wind down the window first?

Certainly if you get married on that basis, real communication may take years or may never even happen, because it's never been learnt in those precious early months. Sex, no matter how good, may keep the relationship going, but it's no substitute for communication and there will inevitably be times when sex isn't happening. What happens then, big boy?

Some blokes will be thinking at this point, 'Come on, being married to me, she won't be able to help herself – it'll be every night!' No, actually it probably won't. It won't because some nights one of you won't be there, or one of you may get ill, or you're both dog-tired, or you've not made up after a row, or strange things like periods happen, or even stranger things like babies pop out – the list is endless.

At all these times your relationship will rely on whatever self-control you've learnt in the years you're in right now. Self-control is a precious gift to be received, and a skill to be learnt, and because so many men have never seen the need for it, crucially when they do need to use self-control, it may not be there to be had. (Unlike some girl in the office.) They're smashing windows and gulping in fresh air all over the place. And another trusting relationship slips quietly over the horizon of betrayal towards the dark waters of divorce.

But enough of the future and back to the boner! I apologize for the heading of the following section, but it seemed there was no other contender for the title. Let's look at the top 10 ways to get out of this kind of trouble. Basically the following suggestions are useful ways of keeping an erection under wraps. If you succeed in this area, you may not have fewer hard-ons, but your girlfriend (or worse, her Mum!) will be none the wiser...

ERECTION SECTION

Chop it off

You could call this a short, sharp introduction, because it will become shorter and will definitely need a sharp implement. A bit drastic though! It's also, I believe, a very unhelpful literal interpretation of Jesus' words from Matthew 18:8: 'If your hand or your foot causes you to sin, cut it off and throw it away.' I believe that Jesus was using this typically Jewish form of exaggeration to show the stuck-up Pharisees that they should do anything rather than miss out on the offer of eternal life. But back to the fleshly life...

Tape it down

Before attempting a tender touch with your partner, have the foresight to tape down the old trouser snake. Use a flexible amount of tape that will 'go with the grow' if this occurs. Otherwise the sound of ripping tape or ripping flesh may be too much to bear, and will definitely cause a suitably off-putting distraction.

Strap it up

A popular alternative, this one. Good quality pants are vital. Such undergarments not only effectively keep everything in order, but by clever use of the elasticated waistband, you have an extra method. Simply skilfully tuck any developing erection underneath the elasticated waistband. The band will then do the job for you. If, however, you return to a seated position, remember to sit down slowly after completing this manoeuvre, or you may temporarily lose the power of speech. Remember: saggy boxer shorts will not work at all.

Pocket battleships

Tried and trusted by thousands. Shove your hands into your pockets, or just the one pocket for a more casual,

'I've got this thing under control' approach. Then make a fist, thereby concealing the problem, and keep the hand there until the emergency subsides.

Freeze (1)

This method is only useful when you're standing up. Once the problem is initially detected, simply remain in exactly the same upright position (that's on your feet) until you find yourself back 'at ease'. Concentrate totally on something un-sexy to take your mind off the problem (e.g. the medicinal properties of cabbage). Remember the catchphrase: Minimum Movement, Maximum Modesty.

Freeze (2)

This is a mobile version of the time-honoured cold shower routine. You need to be somewhere near a handy ice-bucket or tray of watery ice-cubes. Pretend to slip and chuck the whole lot all over the front of your trousers. Ouch! Immediately grab for the nearest towel. Perhaps practise positioning a handy towel nearby before execution. Because of the difficult consequences of this action, it should only be considered when a spare pair of trousers is easily accessible. Do *not* allow your girlfriend to help with the towel in drying you off.

Baggy (1)

Wear baggy trousers, or a baggy jumper or shirt which will hide anything dodgy. Very popular.

Baggy (2)

A personal favourite. Never be without a carrier bag or two which you can use to hold at the appropriate height in front of you as you move, or even as you stand. Standing stationary in the middle of the sitting room while holding a carrier bag is likely to attract comment, however. Skilful adaptations involve pillows, discarded jumpers or coats.

Double up (1)

Wear two pairs of trousers or, for complete peace of mind, a full wet suit under your outer clothes. The secret here is that no one must know you have two layers of clothes on, as the accompanying confession to any discovery may well prove counterproductive.

Double up (2)

Finally, and drastically, when caught out by an erection, pretend to go down with nasty stomach cramps. This involves you bending over at the waist and causing a distraction with your clasped hands. Keep writhing around if you get unhelpful attention from the concerned female who actually caused the problem in the first place. If all else fails, rush for the toilet. An alternative is the 'death drop' onto the floor (face down of course). Please, however, keep this for a dire emergency!

Some of you lads out there may have your own favourites which you could write down and send us, but before we go we can't leave willies behind without confronting two big lies about men's willies that you may well have heard, or even fallen for. Hopefully that should change after you've read what follows.

(1) Blokes can't be cruelly deprived once they've got an erection

As I hope you've sussed out by reading this chapter, having an erection isn't like lighting a firework, i.e., once it's started there's nothing you can do but wait for the explosion! No, an erection is pleasurable, but blokes can have one easily without needing to have an ejaculation, or 'coming' as everyone who doesn't have the letters 'Dr' in front of their name calls it.

Now just supposing one of you reading this book says, 'What's "coming"?' and you're not just referring to the latest film releases – I'm sorry, but I've already said enough about the male sexual organs to fill an entire staffroom with acutely embarrassed PSE (Personal and Social Education) teachers. If you still don't know about the birds and the bees (or, as it should more accurately be known, the birds and the blokes) then I suggest you go up to one of your parents straight away and say in a loud voice, 'Mumsy, how exactly did I get here?' and leave it to them...

Where were we? Oh yes, blokes were designed to have erections. Lots of which will never go anywhere. They can have one for many minutes, even in some cases hours, which doesn't actually mean they have to 'come' at the end. If a bloke has to back off, calm down and have his willy return to its normal size, it's not at all harmful.

He won't black out, go blind, or lose his mind. It may be annoying, but it's similar to how a car driver would feel having to stop the car at a red light if they thought they could sail through on the green. If I said stopping at a red light was damaging to a car, I hope you'd laugh at me. Equally, it isn't harmful having an erection that has to stop. The guy may get all irritated and grumpy at being 'let down', but it has far more to do with what he was expecting than with what's actually happening to him physically: in his head he was already having sex, and he was just waiting for his body to catch up!

(2) Once cruelly deprived, there's an unbearable build-up of pressure

Ah yes, the old 'Exploding Balls' argument! Girls, don't ever say that blokes aren't clever! What a convenient argument this one is – I wonder who thought this one up? (If you don't understand irony, I'm sorry.)

This is a bit like one of those footballer's dives into the penalty box when the defender didn't even touch him. It stinks of cheating and an attempt to con. It's blatant, deserves a booking, but sometimes it actually works. However, if you're a girl, and a bloke has told you that he's had a hard-on for ages which you've caused, and if you don't help 'relieve the pressure' then his balls will ache uncontrollably, don't blow that whistle: show him the red card! You're either going out with the wrong bloke, or you've been repeatedly doing something that you know wasn't helpful ... or I'm afraid you're just plain 'Game for a Laugh' and really need help with your own sense of self-worth.

Whichever way it's tried on you, his balls definitely won't explode, no matter how many unfulfilled erections he may have. He may get a little bit of a pain, but if that's all he's interested in, then he's probably a little bit of a pain anyway. You should politely dump him. This may teach him to respect girls. He can then go off and do what blokes have done to themselves with their spare hand for centuries. Nuff said?

Finally, here's a verse that sums up how each and every Christian should look at this issue of temptation: 'No temptation has seized you except what is common to man.' I'm sure some of you have felt seized Big Time, so you can agree with that bit. But the verse goes on to say this: 'And God is faithful; he will not let you be tempted beyond what you can bear' (1 Corinthians 10:13). If what you're doing with your girlfriend is proving to be beyond what you can bear, it may be many things, but one thing's for sure – God didn't make you do it!

5

YOU mUSt Be YoKinG!

On *A Question of Sport*, the legendary TV quiz show, there's always a round called 'What Happened Next?' and that's really the subject of this chapter. What happens when you find someone, and suddenly the relationship has got very serious? And what if you find that you're getting very serious with someone who isn't really a Christian at all? Maybe they told you a whole bunch of stuff, but only because they were mad keen on you. What happens then? What happens when everything else feels so right – what then?

In my case, when I think of being 18, the one thing I still feel good about was that I did the right thing with the girl I went out with for the whole of that year. Now you may be saying to yourself, 'Hold on. Eighteen-year-old ginger. Bit of a dodgy afro. Bit of a dodgy todger. Christian. It's not a lot to go on, is it?' Well, OK, but at least I hated open-toed sandals! And I was really going for it in my faith, so life was sorted. I had lots of girls who were mates at the time. So, 'What Happened Next?'

This is going to sound so unbelievably cheesy you'll wonder if by accident you just wandered into a cheese shop, but I met this girl – and she wasn't ginger haired! It was the start of a relationship where the two of us felt so complete when we were together that it was scary. It certainly scared her Dad ... one glance at my ginger mophead, and he thought he was going to lose the apple of his eye to a Cox's Orange Pippin!

He was a clever bloke, her Dad. Whenever we used to kiss in my car – not me and him, you under-stand, but me and his daughter – he had this uncanny ability always to be walking the dog past at that point, just casually checking the level of steamed-upness on the car windows. I always thought this ability was remarkable, particularly because, to my knowledge, they didn't actually own a dog.

This girl was a believer, but she was also beautiful. What a bonus! Like all good Christian blokes, I'd put in my order to God for a babe-tastic Christian, and then just waited. While waiting, I worried that God might misunderstand my requests for a strong Christian as being someone who could open beer bottles with her teeth, but I waited all the same. To my delight, she fitted my prayer requests perfectly. However, I also know that some who pray for a 'committed' Christian as a boyfriend or girlfriend only find out later that 'committed' is exactly what they should be, due to the fact that they're several epistles short of a New Testament. I understand. It's tough finding good-looking, well-balanced, cool Christians.

It's even tougher trusting that God is doing the looking for you, and waiting for whoever turns up. It's like trying to find an empty kebab shop at pub-closing time. So what do you do? Do you just go out with Christians, or do you stop being so fussy, as long as they look good and are nice to you? Basically, in a nutshell, if you go out with someone who's not a believer, it can never be the same as if you're both Christians. Never. Some of you might be thinking, 'Thank goodness for that!' but actually your choice isn't just as simple as who's better looking. It's tempting to think that it is, but it's actually more than that. Simply put, it comes down to how important Jesus is to you.

If you choose to go out with a non-Christian, then it may seem at the start like you have so much in common without bringing your faith into it. Therefore you don't need to. You probably already have masses to talk about: friends, music, gossip, films, food, whatever, but as you get to know them better, it dawns on you that the most important thing that you've got going for you – your faith – isn't included. And there's more than that. You realize there's a part of them that just isn't there. Dormant, shut down, whatever it is, their spirit isn't up there yet. Their spirit isn't where yours is, because yours is alive since Jesus started living in your heart. In John 3:6 Jesus puts it like this: 'Flesh gives birth to flesh, but the [Holy] Spirit gives birth to spirit.' That's where it comes from.

They may be fun, and they may be drop-dead gorgeous, so what happens next? If you decide you can't give them up, you may well go for Plan B: conversion. This looks to be a doubly cunning plan, because not only will you get to keep them, but you're also helping God improve his image! You reason to yourself that single-handedly you'll alter God's profile. No more sad geeks with an unnatural urge to wear anoraks – even while indoors. No, from now on, if you convert them, God will be forever grateful. So you get to kill two birds with one stone. You get the relationship you want, plus everybody in church will love you, because this amazing person will become a Christian through you. Top plan!

But there's still more. If you have the imagination to conjure this one up, you'll know that by now this very special friend will be so grateful for your invaluable help in seeing them sorted that marriage is inevitable. Just around the corner. And all because you knew that if you went out, you could convert them. From that day, you'll start a huge ministry to young people together, and take over from Richard and Judy as daytime TV gurus. Tesco will outbid Sainsbury's in getting you to open supermarkets, and you'll be asked to start the Lottery balls rolling. Isn't life fantastic!

Whoops! Just got a bit carried away there. And so might you. The reality may be slightly different. For starters, it takes faith to become a Christian, and that's not something you can give a person, no matter how much you might want to. Equally, even if you could see how much good it would do them, you alone will never be able to just conjure up faith for them. The way I read the Bible, it says that Jesus is 'the author and perfecter of our faith' (Hebrews 12:2), and so we ourselves don't just persuade people into God's kingdom, simply because that's what we want for them. It's basically between them and Jesus.

Most non-Christians who end up going out with Christians are quite happy to talk about God, Jesus and stuff. However, isn't it funny that the sort of persuading they suddenly find themselves needing, curiously, only seems able to be done down the pub on a Sunday night? If you're a Christian this can cause you a dilemma, because often that's the night when you should get together for your youth group session.

What do you do? Well, what often happens is that you tell yourself that on this particular night, this special person is much more important than sitting reading a dry old bit of Galatians. So you skip your youth group – in the belief that you're genuinely doing God's will – and tell yourself that you'll look at that passage later. This way, you won't actually miss anything. All I'd like to say is this: nice intention, but let me give you a dry old bit of Galatians. 'But watch yourself, or you also may be tempted' (6:1).

The first time you miss your Christian group, you think hard about your decision. The next week, however, it gets a little easier; the week after that a bit easier still, and so on. Before you know where you are, you haven't met with your youth group for a month, and if you've got the guts to take a hard look at it, your special friend hasn't asked many questions about God recently either. In fact, the only one who appears to have benefited during these last few weeks is the pub landlord! If at this point your Christian leader hasn't even noticed or said anything, you feel justified in staying away. 'No one bothered when I wasn't there,' you think, 'so why should I bother going again now?'

I'm not having a pop at pubs. After all, part of your reasons for being there, if you're a Christian, are entirely good: 'Always be prepared to give an answer to everyone who asks you to give the reason for the hope that you have' (1 Peter 3:15). But forget your fellow Christians at your peril. You need them more if you're going out with a non-Christian than you ever did before. If you don't see them on Sundays for spiritual support, when else are you going to do it? And not just to say 'Hi' and catch up, but to continue to grow.

The easiest way to describe what's happening here is that your love life may be going swimmingly, but what you might have ended up demonstrating by the choices you make on a day-to-day basis is that your need of Jesus isn't very, well, needy. So your girlfriend or boyfriend ends up thinking almost sub-consciously: 'If this Christian shows they don't actually need Jesus, yet they're still saying they do – where does that leave me? I may be needy, but if they can live without it, then so can I.' You may have told your partner already that faith is really important to you, which was great. And you may also have been brave enough to tell them they need Jesus too – but are you 'walking the talk'?

Then, on top of that, you add this problem. Your new special friend appears to be just so gobsmackingly nice! In fact, they seem to be a nicer person than you! You look at them, and you notice that their concern for their mates, for their family, for the environment, for lesser spotted whales, whatever, may be on a level that puts your God stuff in the shade. It feels, in comparison, like you're really only playing at it.

To make matters worse, your parents, even Christian parents, are so relieved that you're not going out with someone who tortures ponies for kicks, they become suddenly, sickeningly nice back. Your boyfriend or girlfriend now thinks they're on to a winner, and flashes your parents the same winning smile that won your heart. Everyone is laughing. Unfortunately, this makes it even more difficult for your friend to believe they may need saving, because inside them a logical little voice is saying, 'Wait a minute, everybody loves me, nobody hates me. So where's the problem?'

Well, the Book of Jeremiah for one says this: 'The heart is deceitful above all things. Who can understand it?' (17:9) No one wants to hear that they aren't all they crack themselves up to be. But if everything else that's being communicated to them, by your friends, by your family, even by you, says that they're actually fine and dandy the way they are, then it gets difficult. Hey, so long as they turn on the charm, even your pets think they're the bee's knees!

This is one main reason why trying to preach to your non-Christian boyfriend or girlfriend proves so very difficult. Even saying they need Jesus seems to sound a tad hollow, so why bother? Simple. Because it's got to be done. But you may not be the one to do it. You didn't become a Christian because you were nice, or because you weren't. You became a Christian because you knew in your heart that you needed Jesus. And so do they. That's why it's only the Holy Spirit who really convicts people, not you. Your job is to pray that they will receive him.

But remember: other Christians may well be praying for the two of you ... Imagine the scenario: You bump into some worthy churchy types who know you. They start chatting a bit awkwardly, the conversation meanders inconclusively along, and then without any warning at all, they lob a biblical hand grenade in your direction, talking about yokes and oxen and ploughing! You look very confused. You are very confused. You want to say, 'I haven't got a Scoobie Doo what's going on here,' but instead you just smile back. They tell you it's from 2 Corinthians 6:14. You promise to go home and think about it. The verse says this: 'Do not be yoked together with unbelievers.'

This verse has been used by many Christians to indicate that it's impossible to have a committed relationship with someone who doesn't believe. Being yoked together is how all farming was done before tractors, and if you have two oxen sharing the same yoke but pulling in different directions, then the furrow they plough will be all over the place. So the verse was very graphic for all those who lived on the land then, and for those who still do. It can also be very helpful, because the universal truth is that if you want to get anything right in a partnership, you need to be compatible, both pulling together in the same direction. It's not, as one of my youth group once told me, 'just a load of bullocks'!

'Oh,' I can hear you saying as the light dawns, 'but wait a minute, I don't want to plough a furrow with my partner, or with anyone else for that matter. In fact, I don't want to be involved with any heavy farming implements, thank you.' Then, if you're thinking fast, you may say that if this verse is about being yoked together, it must be standing for the Big M: marriage. Finally, you add that you have no intention of being married yet, so that lets you off the hook, right? Well, if this was a tennis match, you'd have won the point, but you haven't yet won the game.

Of course this verse includes those who are thinking of getting married, but it can also include you if you're serious about someone who isn't a Christian. So the question to both of you is: Are you, together, aiming for the same things? And just as you're thinking about that, if you carry on reading the verse, it slaps you round the kisser thus: 'For what do right-eousness and wickedness have in common? Or what fellowship can light have with darkness?' Pardon? You've just been Tangoed!

It's understandable if you get defensive at this type of black-and-white approach. How can they call the one you love 'darkness'? I expect, if you feel like fighting back, you'd say that you know couples going out seriously who say they're Christians, yet you've seen what they get up to. You'll say that they never talk about Jesus or pray together. Therefore, you argue, they're no better. Indeed, they may be worse. 'If loving you is wrong, I don't want to be right ...' could be how you feel. Yet the biblical ideal stands. It's saying that unless you do something about it, your partner can easily drain away your spiritual life. You might even be floundering right now because of it.

So if you really want to love your boyfriend or girl-friend, and you really want to love Jesus as well, are you setting yourself up for an impossible love triangle? Well, let's talk triangles for a minute. Experience tells us that some triangles are stable and look right. Others are unstable and look wrong. A triangle that looks right could include one summing up our relationships. It will have Jesus at one point, and the two of you at the other two points. If you both move closer to Jesus, the points of the triangle move closer to each other. The brilliant result is that the two of you move closer to each other as well! If, however, the two of you move closer together, but Jesus can't move closer to your partner, then the triangle begins to look decidedly odd. It's simply because you just can't keep two wholehearted relationships going at the same time if they're headed in different directions. Ask anyone.

Ask a bloke or a girl who you know is two-timing their partner. It always results in big-time deceit going on. If you don't believe me just watch Jerry Springer on TV sometime. You end up with some very odd-shaped relationships, and some of those triangles on TV are weird, man! Personally I know because I went out with a strong Christian when I wasn't, and I nearly killed her faith off. But wait a minute, that's a later story, and we should return to the cheesy girl I was talking about at the start of this chapter, because at that time Jesus was the most important person to me, and she knew it, and fantastically, she felt the same way. We had a good, cheesy triangle!

So although we spent hours together finding out about each other's lives, ideas and dental work, and although we struggled with temptation to take it further, we never did. We kept Jesus in, which helped keep our clothes on! There may be some of you who can't quite believe that it's possible not to let the physical side of the relationship completely dominate everything, but it is. Not because I just say so, but because lots of people who've joined True Love Waits have told me so. The key to it has to be that you're just going to have to do things together where the focus isn't solely on each other. Keep that triangle going, and show how thankful you are for what God has given the two of you, by giving out a bit of what's left over to other people. Let's give it a dodgy title: let's call it a love tithe!

When you go out with someone and your love for that other person becomes all-consuming, it's actually love with little risk. You know you give, but you also know that you'll get back too. It just goes round and round in a safe little circle between the two of you. There are no risks involved. No-risk loving is definitely love with a little 'l'. The only real risk in that sort of relationship is whether another member of the family comes back early to disturb the two of you on the sofa!

Jesus' love for us was a Big Love, so you could live in a way that's other than selfish. Now that you've read this chapter I can confidently advise that a Big Love triangle has got to be the best way going. If, however, you've just opened the book at this bit and read the words 'Big Love triangle', you're going to think that I'm definitely out to lunch with the fairies. My advice to you, therefore, is to start at the beginning, keep Jesus in, keep your clothes on, and may all your triangles be a lot less cheesy than mine!

6

ThE FutuRe's bRighT,
THE FUTURE'S ORANGE

One day I got a letter from my Miss Cheese. It was a
'Dear Jon' letter. We'd been as close as Mr B and Mr Q
when they started out in business, but suddenly with
the arrival of my 'Dear Jon' letter I was dumped with a
capital 'D'. That year wasn't a great year for me. I got
a 'Dear Jon' letter from my work too. This was particularly hard to take as my boss was a Christian trying to
run a Christian business – without me.

Then I got a 'Dear Jon' letter from my church. The

pastor said, 'Son, you'll always be a quitter,' and I wasn't even a smoker! Then my flat and my car both got badly damaged. In the case of the flat it was done by hooligans, and in the case of the car it was done by yours truly. I parked a large company van in the same space where my car had been quietly minding its own business, and two into one definitely didn't fit! To quote the Queen: *Annus Pigus Sickus*.

There was nothing else for it. I looked at the evidence in front of me and, like Laurel and Hardy, told God, 'That's another fine mess you've got me into!' This wasn't fair on him, but then things weren't exactly fine and dandy from where I was sitting either. All the frustration and hurt that I felt over those events built up and built up within me. I didn't take them to the Lord in prayer, I felt isolated by the attitude of the church, and I wasn't at all comforted by that 'Footsteps' poem that talks about Jesus carrying us when life is hardest. Even though I'd been so sorted as a Christian before, it all suddenly felt like a load of twaddle.

I decided it was time to say 'Goodbye God'. After all, I reckoned he was doing a less effective job as supposed boss of my life than a hatful of sacked football managers. The hardest thing, I felt, was that Jesus was out there somewhere, but he didn't seem the least bit bothered by the state I was in. In fact, far from loving me, I felt that if we were to meet face to face I'd be saying, 'Remember me?' and he'd be replying, 'Nope. I'm awfully sorry, but I just can't place you.' After that it was easy to say 'Goodbye God'. And once you've said that, 'Hello Girls!' usually follows.

I gave up work and became an arty-farty actor. I needed to 'find myself'. I also figured out that I needed to find a new girlfriend. Jesus talked about leaving the disciples 'another Comforter' because he knew all of us, even tough old fishermen or hairy Hell's Angel bikers, need comforting. It's just a basic human need, and boy, was I in need of it.

The Holy Spirit is able to meet that need, but a lot of people – including me at the time – only look for that comfort in the closeness of another human being. That's why, when that closeness becomes a sexual thing, lots of non-Christians have a real problem if you then start talking about it as sin. How, they ask, can we possibly tell someone else that they shouldn't have such basic human closeness? After all, they say, isn't it a fundamental right that everyone should be entitled to?

Because of this problem, the good old Church of England was forced to abandon the expression 'living in sin' in exchange for being seen (they hoped) as much more understanding. However, just changing the words wasn't going to help; that's not where we get our comfort from. The Holy Spirit is given to believers with a job to do, and a big part of his job description lies right here (John 16:7).

Unfortunately I wasn't looking to him. Instead I was looking for a girl, and I found one. It wasn't true love. It was just two needy people who wouldn't let Jesus help. Inevitably I guess, given that background, we ended up sleeping together. Reading this may make stacks of you throw this book across the room shouting, 'You ginger hypocrite!' and if that's the case I may well deserve it. It isn't a memory I cherish and I'm not proud of myself, nor do I feel, like some do, that there should be nothing you regret. This I regret.

It has, however, made me what I am today: determined that you should never have sex because you think it'll meet all your needs – like physical ones, which I guess are the most obvious, then those needs for self-worth where feelings and emotions meet, and finally those needs where the emotional and spiritual join to make you the unique You that no one else shares. In reality it'll probably do just one of those, and any businessman will tell you that a 33 per cent return for a 100 per cent investment is a mug's game.

For me it was simply the result of kicking Jesus out of the driver's seat, and shoving him out of sight into the boot. I was a mixed-up bloke who figured I'd given it my best shot – and by then I was 21, so what the heck. She was very sweet to me, even though I was too preoccupied to help *her* much, and for that I still cringe inside. How selfish I was! I was like someone stumbling around in the dark looking for a light at the end of a tunnel, and the only light I could see was the minister of the church shining a torch at me to see if I'd quit yet. I quit.

I settled for second best because I wasn't sure any more what 'best' was supposed to be. I did decide, however, that I would conduct an experiment. I would now live my life by *my* rules for the next few years, and see if I could do a better job than God.

Not a bad experiment, I thought. After all, if God could make such a mess, I had to be in with a shout.

I started off well. By the age of 23 I thought I'd cracked it. I had a smooth company car, a slick company suit, a fat company pay packet, a new racy girlfriend, and I raced a new racy racing car. Yes, it was life in the fast lane for me. I did keep my Christian insurance policy going by having a girlfriend who was a Christian, but I ended up stringing her along with tales of how I'd like to get God back into my life sometime.

I now held onto that oh-so-popular belief, the 'Deathbed Apology'. This involves living a life packed brim-full of general naughtiness, and then slipping sweetly into a coma with the words 'Sorry God' on your lips, and everything will be cushy! In the end, as I fear is the case for the vast majority, my quest for naughtiness was my undoing. I two-timed the Christian, and if that sounds horrible it probably sums up my behaviour at the time.

Then I bought a house and moved in with someone completely different (keep a note of her, she reappears later). Unfortunately this turned out to be a seriously dumb idea. Dumb because we naively intended to be oh-so-mature about these things. It was supposed to be primarily a financial arrangement whereby we both made a bit of money out of the house, and enjoyed ourselves along the way. Dumb idea. Dumber timing.

My thinking was now about as straight as the Leaning Tower of Pisa, and I stumbled into the 1990s feeling that life had somehow short-changed me. Besides, I hadn't had my naughty quota for the decade, yet somehow I'd ended up with more grief than I'd bargained for. I was confused, angry and unrepentant. It was never like this in the movies.

Finally I decided that I was going to cut my losses in the God-links department and move in with someone new. Perhaps this girl was The One. This girl didn't have a faith at all. She thought 'Faith' was a hit song by George Michael. This girl would do for me all the things my naughty quota demanded. It was 'Goodbye God' for good. I made this very clear and definite decision in my head, expecting to act on it the next morning. I thought that the next day was to be one that would change my life forever, but I hadn't counted on what God might have in mind. My life was indeed just about to change forever...

God decided it was time to blow the whistle on me. Enough was enough. It was time I came back home. Aptly, he blew the whistle on me in a football match. That morning I played football as I usually did at weekends, and as the game got going, I thought I was playing a blinder. Or, to be more accurate, I was just about to! The advice to 'keep your eye on the ball' was about to take a hideous twist.

As I ran in to play a header, unbeknown to me the other bloke thought he might fancy a flashy, continental-style overhead kick. To his credit he got full contact with the ball. The trouble was, it was the wrong ball. Having smacked the ball as hard as he could, he might have been disappointed not to see the football flash into the net. I was, perhaps, slightly more disappointed, on account of the ball he hit having been, up until that point, my eyeball. This was not helpful.

I knew from the pain that this was also Serious Trouble. I was too frightened to put my finger in the place where my eye might have been, just in case it wasn't there any more. Fortunately it was, though badly misshapen, and with the imprint of the end of his boot on it. My eye itself was also bleeding, and the bone of my eye socket took such an impact that it chipped a lump clean off. So there was both good news and bad news. The bad news was that I was blind. The good news was that we went on to win. Tactical substitution, I call it.

My first reaction: 'Everybody stand still and don't tread on my eye!' was quickly followed by my second: This was God's doing! Vindictive and nasty was not, however, how I felt God met me that day. The words, 'Those I love, I reprove and discipline' (Revelation 3:19) came to mind, and moments before my body went into limb-wobbling shock, I also felt God was telling me something about Samson, the Old Testament character.

This all happened very soon after the impact, but it obviously took a while before the meaning truly began to sink in. Perhaps the blindness was the link with Samson? Or the dodgy hair thing? I waited to find out what it was. As you can imagine, other more immediate concerns were uppermost in my mind right then.

7

MY OWN PERSONAL
DELILAH

Mercifully I was only temporarily blinded, but I couldn't
open either of my eyes at all for over two weeks
because of the wicked pain when my bad eye automatically tried to focus as I was trying to use my good
one. So I just lay in bed, blind. You should try it sometime (no, not lying in bed for days, but being confined
to darkness for a while). It certainly makes you think.
Even if my eyes couldn't focus, my thoughts certainly
could, and I realized I desperately needed sorting out.

Anyone who comes back to God, just like it says in the story of the returning Prodigal Son, realizes they need forgiveness. Yet this is also very much a two-way street. Jesus taught us to pray, 'Forgive us our sins, as we forgive those who sin against us.' He couldn't have made it any clearer, even if the sins we need to forgive others for may be more to do with how we see things than what actually took place. In my case, as I lay there I realized I needed to forgive the girl I'd lived with in the house, because I held some pretty hefty grudges against her. In the darkness I pictured her and I imagined saying the words to her: 'I completely forgive you.' As I did that, God forgave me.

My sight slowly returned. The first time I could open the Bible I thought I'd better get to the bottom of this Samson thing. I didn't know where Samson was in the Bible, but conveniently for me the Bible opened at the very page the first time I looked for it. This was spooky, as I hadn't even looked up the page number beforehand. I knew that I had to be getting warm. Now, as I read about Samson's life, I began to realize how amazing his story was, and how relevant to me it all became.

I suggest you have a look at the whole thing, but I really think Samson has a message for people who say, in the words of the song by those old rockers Queen, 'I want it all, and I want it now!' He was just like that. He was also very definitely an impressive bloke. He was chosen by God to rule over the Israelites even before he was born, and he did this quite successfully for 20 years. It was a rough, tough time and it suited a rough, tough leader. He must have looked a bit of a wild man as well because of his long, flowing hair which he'd sworn never to cut. Think of 'Wolf' off *Gladiators* – and then some! He had one weakness, though. He apparently had no idea how to control himself, and I'm not talking about his bladder, I'm talking about his hormones.

This showed itself in several ways, but his red-hot weakness was sex – he was indeed a true ladies' man. I can just see him with a big gold medallion, hairy chest, silk shirt open to the navel, sitting in an Essex winebar, winking suggestively at the girls... Funny choice for a leader, you may be thinking. God had called him and anointed him, and yet you take one look and you think 'Why? Wasn't there anyone

else better qualified, God?' Or is the story of Samson
there for the benefit of people like you and me today,
who struggle with how blessing and bonking go
together?

Essex Girl didn't exist in those days, but they did
have the saucy, suggestive Philistine Filly! Samson,
don't forget, was to lead God's people against their
old enemy the Philistines, yet in the bits we get to
read, Samson seems to spend his entire time sniffing
around such teasing tottie. An insight into what makes
him tick is the fact that instead of doing the normal
thing and letting his parents choose a suitable wife,
Samson lets his eyes do the choosing. Put it this way,
I don't think Samson was thinking much about a meeting of minds.

So he gets his way. But like most relationships
built on physical attraction alone, things start to go
wrong quite early on. He's definitely still at first base
on the commitment thing. Even during the wedding
he storms off in such a huff that his new dad-in-law
thinks he must despise his new wife, so when Samson
doesn't reappear he lets her go off with someone
else. Much later we see a calmed-down Samson

return, ready to get down to action in the bedroom as if nothing's happened. Unfortunately it's all gone pear-shaped (unlike his wife's figure) in his absence.

Now get this: he's God's man, he's the one who's been chosen by God to lead his people, he's the one who knows a big-time calling on his life, yet we find dad-in-law talking to this great man of God as follows. 'I was so sure you thoroughly hated her,' he says, 'that I gave her to your friend. Isn't her younger sister more attractive? Take her instead.' Doesn't that make Samson sound a sleaze?

Samson can't help himself now. If he was upset before, you haven't seen what mayhem he's about to unleash. He's a one-man race riot. Of course, like most people in this frame of mind, it never occurs to him that he might have been responsible in some way for some of the pear-shapedness. Oh no. Yet, amazingly, God doesn't take his blessing away. Perhaps this is the beginning of the end for Samson. However, his wandering eyes, which got him into that mess to start with, aren't finished yet.

To take his mind off his domestic problems, he goes off again, risking life and limb for a different bit of Philistine crumpet. Again he somehow squeaks through that one unscathed, and we still haven't met Delilah yet! Suddenly, there she is. Like one of those animal cartoons where the animal leaps into the air with its tongue hanging out, fireworks going off, and cupid's love-hearts in its eyes, Samson thinks he's found his perfect lady at last.

Now Samson's reactions may, perhaps, have been fine and dandy if he was just another good-looking Jew, but remember who he was. He still has God's anointing, but despite all his near misses with young Philistine misses, he's quite happy to get into this relationship without thinking about what might happen to God's blessing. The trouble is, he's relied on it being there so often in the past that he simply assumes it will always carry on that way. So, like a small child with a box of matches, first of all he just holds the box, then he just opens the box, then he just takes out a match, then he just practises lighting it, and then he gets burnt. Badly.

If you've ever played with matches as a kid, you'll know that at each of those stages you could be told off, and if you're feeling stroppy, you could say, 'But I'm not doing anything, I'm just holding them, I'm not actually going to light one...' Well, it was sort of the same with Samson. At any point he could have said, 'But I'm not doing anything, and I'm not actually going to lose the anointing, so stop going on...' The trouble was, as Delilah got more and more under his skin, Samson was prepared to take more and more risks with that blessing and take it more and more for granted.

So he was prepared to compromise and compromise, getting nearer and nearer to giving away the secret of his strength, but not actually losing it, until finally he put a greater price on keeping Delilah happy than on his relationship with God. In the end, it was just too much effort. Poor old Samson. 'Love is blind,' as they say, but he should have seen it coming. In his case love was very definitely about to become blind.

How was I like Samson, then? Strong, handsome, rugged, resourceful ... sorry about that, just got a bit carried away! No, seriously, apart from the fact that we both had silly hair, there is something else. God had very definitely blessed me when I was a teenager, and yet I wasn't satisfied with that. When things got tough, instead of realizing that God uses tough times to make us more like Jesus, I took the easy way out. Like Samson I assumed I could return any time I wanted, and God's blessings would be sitting there waiting for my return. However, after a while you just don't value the blessing as highly, in fact you're prepared each time to go that little bit further, then a little bit further still. Like an endless elastic band, you assume God's grace can be stretched and stretched and stretched.

God's grace *is* very stretchy, but what happened to Samson is what also happened to me. Instead of his grace snapping, you end up simply not being bothered any more, and so you take the scissors to it yourself. Just like they cut Samson's hair off because he couldn't be doing with the effort it was taking to keep hold of both God and the girl in his life at the same time. I was like that because I, too, wanted both. But when it came to the crunch and having to choose one or the other, sadly I just wanted the girl.

Perhaps you know what I'm talking about. You've had God's blessing in a powerful way in your life, but that may have been a while ago. Now you're not quite sure whether it's as important to you as it once was and something, or more usually, *someone* new has come along – your own personal Delilah. Little by little, even if you don't intend to throw it out, it just slides slowly away, like poor old Leonardo di Caprio into the Atlantic Ocean.

Samson simply couldn't be bothered with it any more. He'd played with the idea of giving it away so many times that in the end it was easy. Like that box of matches, to begin with you never intended to light one, but in the end you've gone so far playing with the idea in your head, and then practising with your hand, that you can't see the point of not actually lighting one. Why not?

As I read these chapters on Samson I recognized how I'd decided just to give God's blessing away without any fuss at all in the end, because I'd been compromising for so long. I was going out with the wrong girl, my own personal Delilah, and at that point God decided enough was enough. I couldn't carry on wasting what he'd given me. 'Those I love I reprove and discipline' was his way of telling me he loved me too much to stand by and watch that happen. How I'd chosen to live actually bothered him enough for him to do something, to intervene. He did actually answer a 21-year-old's prayer – except that by then I was 28!

The final part of Samson's life, however, showed me that there was a Part 2 for me as well. There was one last thing that Samson could do, despite being permanently blinded, and there was one last thing for me to do, despite being temporarily blinded.

What was it that Samson did? Well, it was pretty dramatic! He was chained in the basement of his enemies' palace, mocked by his enemies as a fool, yet at last we can see him doing what he should have done all along: humbly praying to his God. As his strength slowly returned, with one huge effort he pulled the whole thing down on his head, flattening himself and the Philistine posse in the process. It was either dodgy DIY from those Philistines, or God's blessing had very definitely returned. Otherwise such strength could only be put down to an awful lot of Popeye's spinach!

In my case, God was graciously showing me I could have a second go, but that like Samson, that was really it. I'm not saying this would be the message for others, but it was the message for me. I suppose I'm so thick that I needed to know I couldn't just have any number of stabs at it. It was a little bit of a warning, I guess, because this time it mattered, and I mustn't think there were endless other chances if I just let the blessing dribble away again. Gulp!

The first thing I had to do was finish with my own personal Delilah. Then, with all that grot of unforgiveness given the boot, and a fresh dose of forgiveness released through my hours spent in prayer, the girl with the house came back into my head – a bit like the Philistine palace did into Samson's head! In my mind it was like seeing her for the first time all over again, and the bitterness and anger fell off her like, er, like a muddy car being jetwashed clean...

I could once again picture her as she was, the enchanting girl I fell for at the start of what was for both of us a very unhelpful and dodgy relationship. No longer the one I blamed for everything that went wrong, in my mind she'd now changed. Seeing as we'd well and truly split up and weren't speaking, however, I somehow had to find out if things could ever be good again – or was it just wishful thinking induced by a smack on the head with a size 10 Adidas?

Having seen her in my mind, I now wanted to see her with my eyes. The more I thought about her, the more excited I got. Firstly, about seeing her, but also about what we could be together if only we could let God into the relationship this time around. You know how your imagination can completely run away with you if you let it? Now I couldn't help dreaming big dreams of what the two of us could be together.

If God wanted this to happen, and it was meant to be, then I for one was up for it big-time! Good grief, all of a sudden, for the first time in my life, I wanted to marry someone and spend the rest of my life with them. From whichever angle I looked at it, I still felt God's peace about it, and didn't feel at all scared or manoeuvred into this decision by anything other than love and a strong desire. And that desire was to see the best God wanted for me, and to be the best he wanted me to be. The only minor problem I could see was that we weren't even on speaking terms at the time!

I was in the mood for 'The Dramatic Gesture'. I wanted to propose to her as soon as possible. But would she see me? To my delight she was willing to come over and talk. We talked about the accident – it was brilliant! She told me she'd be singing in her church the next week, which was actually Christmas Eve, which also happened to be her birthday. 'Perfect!' I thought. 'I'll slip quietly into the church without her knowing, and like Noel Edmonds on *Noel's House Party* I'll jump out halfway through her song, totally surprising her, propose, and sweep her off her feet!' Fortunately, the lady minister I let in on the plan obviously knew the signs of a size 10 Adidas attack and told me to go home for a little lie down. I complied.

Now I had time to work on Plan B. I called this one 'The Faxed Marriage Proposal'. After all, if we've got the technology, why not use it? December turned to January, and because Joanna didn't have a fax at home, and I thought it was a top plan, I decided to fax her at work instead. The only problem I could foresee was that the fax was shared between her and about half a dozen other women...

It was really fiendishly simple. I got this bloke in a fax bureau to fax over one sheet of paper late one

afternoon, while I skulked about in the shadows outside her office with my mobile phone. In big letters the
fax read, 'WOULD YOU SAY YES'. He then rang to
check that it had landed on Joanna's desk, and not that
of the rather elderly spinster who worked behind the
partition, which would have proved a tad embarrassing. Then he sent the next one. This one read, 'IF I
ASKED YOU'. It was now time for me to spring into
action. With SAS slickness, I nonchalantly entered the
building carrying the third and final sheet of fax paper.

The third fax definitely needed delivering by
hand. I got a rather puzzled receptionist to ring up to
Joanna's office and tell her there was a fax waiting
downstairs which she needed to collect. This was it!
Upstairs things were happening too. Being a smart
cookie, Joanna had realized something odd was
going on, and was causing some alarm because she
started applying make-up while telling her amused
colleagues that she thought she was being proposed
to by fax. To them, of course, faxes were clever things,
but they still couldn't work out why putting make-up
on should make any difference to the fax roll. At least
it brightened up a dreary winter's afternoon...

Downstairs I decided to surprise Joanna by being on one knee when she came out of the lift. I got down on one knee, the lift door opened – and the bloke who filled up the drinks machine in the office nearly fell over me. Unperturbed, I waited for the lift a second time. This time the door opened and ... and nothing! I was proposing undying love to an empty lift. While I was doing this, Joanna had walked down the back stairs and stood quietly behind me, waiting for me to get up. Perhaps I still had something to learn about how the SAS do things. My last fax sheet, which I was clutching between trembling hands, said, 'TO MARRY ME PLEASE?'

Looking back, the whole thing sounds deeply embarrassing, but at least I had a lot to be thankful for; at least it hadn't been the elderly spinster jumping out of the lift and smothering me with kisses!

One week we weren't even friends, the next we were engaged. When Joanna told her sisters she was getting married, their reaction was, 'Great ... who to?' Surprise, shock, delight – it had all happened so quickly, but Joanna and I did things right this time. Now we were looking forward (in my case a bit skewwhiffly with that eye of mine) to the future, but this time with God. Together.

Within four months we were married. Neither of us had wanted to wait the first time around before getting intimate, but this time we waited. Four months isn't very long, and there are some of you out there who've waited an awful lot longer, but we did wait until our marriage night gave us the green light to sleep together. Yum yum! That's the main reason why we decided to have a short engagement, because long engagements don't make too much sense if you know it's right to marry your fiancé(e). Also, please don't let either of your mothers keep you waiting because they want to book some flashy place for the reception! It's your life, so go for it if you know that the three of you (you, your fiancé(e) and God) want it to work. This is the only time when True Love Waits should be renamed True Love Doesn't Hang Around!

8

TrUe LOvE worKs

The fun had just begun. Married life, however, does take time to suss out. Sorry to sound like some boring old footballer trotting out the 'game of two halves' cliché, but you've got to work at it. And it does work better the better you two work. Of course you're in love at the time, but changing together as two people becoming one still results in the odd growing pain or two, no matter who you are. In my case it was helped by stopping being busy as if my life depended on it, and instead starting to learn to depend on God.

One result of this was that in my new-found time off I started doing Christian youth work. I started with five lads. I don't know who was more terrified, these 'Famous Five' or me. But as I prayed, it dawned on me that this was just the start. I told my wife I thought God had a place for me in the church, and it wasn't the fourth pew back on the left!

Just after that the main youth leader asked me to go along to a meeting at which the appointment of a youth worker was to be discussed. I didn't have the sense to ask him where I should go, or when. But seeing as we Christians always either have meetings at 7.45 or 8.00 p.m., I plumped for 7.45. Possibly for the only time ever, I found myself arriving early for something called the PCC (Parochial Church Council) – long before the Vicar of Dibley ever made them fashionable!

They discussed a new appointment within our church of a part-time paid youth worker. I sat there as an invited representative, and by the end I had to contain myself firmly, trying not to shout out, 'It's me! It's me! I can do this!' Fortunately I didn't, because most of them didn't know me from Adam, but as weeks passed 'it came to pass' that, sure enough, 'twas me! The church had the vision to take me on, and my own vision was fortunately once again 20/20. The timing was also sorted, because that first week one boy was arrested for stabbing someone on a school trip, and another lad's father died of a massive heart attack – and that was just out of the Famous Five! Talk about jumping in at the deep end...

In 1994 they made me full time. But even then I still had a problem. The problem reared its ugly head whenever we came to that bit in the teaching programme about sex. I always got so hideously embarrassed, it was embarrassing! 'How can I put them straight,' I thought, 'when I've been pretty wobbly myself?' Yet the issue wouldn't go away. If any youth worker ever says to any group of kids, 'So, what do you want us to do?' it's always the same three subjects that come up: sex, drugs and rock'n'roll! That year we also went along to the big Christian music festival called Greenbelt, and I remember going to a seminar on sex where the grown-up 'experts' were being as broadminded as possible, and yet the teenagers there weren't happy. They didn't go for that – they wanted instead to know exactly where the Bible was coming from, and no messing. This profoundly impressed me.

Late in 1996 my youth group, which is called CPs (stands for Couch Potatoes!), watched a Channel 4 documentary with me on True Love Waits in the United States. Most of them just laughed at those wacky Yanks. However, behind the send-up, I knew that lots of them believed exactly the same message. This bothered me. Not only did it bother me, it made me think about the whole issue over and over again. I became obsessed with sex! I phoned other Christians and talked sex. I couldn't think of anything else for days. Basically the message I kept getting back was, 'Well, nobody's doing anything like that in this country, but if you think it should be done – you'll have to do it yourself!'

So we did! During the next three months, using the wisdom of teenagers who dropped in on our house, we evolved what we wanted the promise material to look like. We wanted something that could be carried around in a wallet or purse, and settled on a credit-card-style piece of plastic, with an all-important signature strip on the reverse. Thirty-two rewrites of the wording later, we finally ended up with something that wasn't too long to read, but included a natty little ditty (calling it a poem sounds too pretentious) which for some reason stuck. We also decided to run the risk of dodgy phonecalls by putting our home phone number on the card. It was now ready.

The only problem was that the card-makers weren't going to make good quality ones in quantities of less than 5,000. Our youth group didn't quite stretch to 5,000 – even when we had 'free food' nights! I'm no mathematician, but I reckoned that 4,970 would still be looking for homes afterwards. Common sense therefore suggested that we'd have to make it nationwide if it was going to happen at all. So we did something silly. We ordered 10,000. Where we were going to find 10,000 strong Christians in the UK prepared to walk around with one of these little cards, heaven only knew, but I ordered them anyway.

As we had no money, this wasn't bad. The ordering was the easy bit; the paying for it – now that was going to be harder! We talked to John Buckeridge, the editor of *Youthwork* magazine, and asked his advice. He took one look at the card and decided that it was bold enough to be stuck on the front cover of February 1997's Valentine's Day edition of the magazine. Then three very generous couples at church got to hear about it and each gave us £500. We'd arrived.

With baited breath we waited for the February edition of *Youthwork* to drop through people's letter-boxes. Wonderfully, the phone started ringing. Other youth workers up and down the country started to phone and write with orders for more cards. People liked them! We were on a roll! Total strangers wrote 'well done, good on ya!' type of letters. We were even surprised by the number of British Christians who were already receiving stuff from True Love Waits in the United States and were delighted to know they could now get their own version. Other Christian organizations in this field wrote to us expressing interest, like Care for the Family, and finally it appeared that the Evangelical Alliance could now say someone was prepared to talk to the media about teenage sex. Hey, we even had a big order from the Seychelles – this thing was international!

By coincidence, *Bliss,* the teenage magazine, then ran a four-page article on True Love Waits in the States, and to give it a bit of balance, quoted the UK Youth Department of the Baptist Union, who said something like this was 'unlikely' to happen in this country. Well, as you can imagine, with us mailing parcels of our cards out just as fast as we could pack them, it would have been better if he'd done his homework first! In the article *Bliss* themselves were a bit naughty with their main caption. It read, 'It's hard to say no when your boyfriend is begging for it', but when you read the interview the girl actually said that she was pleased her Christian boyfriend didn't push for sex, because, '*It must be* hard to say no when your boyfriend is begging for it...'

As you can see, it's an oh-so-subtle difference, but it's there. The caption quote makes her sound like someone who'd like to say 'no', but when it came to the crunch she just couldn't. But she wasn't saying that at all. She was trying to imagine what other girls had to go through if they were with a boyfriend who wouldn't take 'no' for an answer.

We learnt two things from this article: (1) that plenty of Christians in this country have already settled for second place behind 'condom culture', and (2) that the UK media are fascinated by the whole idea of virgins who choose to be virgins. It follows that if they can't find any, they'll end up having their suspicions confirmed that virginity really belongs with other extinct things like Woolly Mammoths and rickets. A bit like the message in a shop window which read, 'Virginity is curable, see inside for details'. It meant we had to think about what to say to the media. Unfortunately, we didn't have a clue where to start. Fortunately, the media started on us.

'Can you do a late-night Friday evening debate next week here in Nottingham led by Nicky Campbell?' the chirpy researcher enquired. At the time it seemed so easy to say 'yes', but we soon realized that they'd made it so we couldn't say 'no'. We got a big, black, chauffeur-driven Mercedes driven to our door, hospitality suite when we got there, and all the drink and food we could wish for.

As I sat in the back with Joe, a trendy 16-year-old, being whisked up the M1, we passed a lorry-load of sheep – and suddenly I understood exactly where we were off to. We were on our way to be slaughtered! Like sacrificial lambs, they'd got a few Christians in, and as the chauffeur told us ghoulish tales of TV torture, we sat there wondering when we'd start to sniff the mint sauce.

We must have looked like TV virgins, too. All wide eyed and a bit too keen with the free drinks. Nicky Campbell's attitude beforehand added to the pressure, and I had visions of Joe being tempted to tuck into the free beers, then staggering out in front of the cameras. Fortunately that didn't happen.

What did happen was that both Joe and I felt a real freedom to talk as committed Christians with the other guests, which was great because they had the lot in that night – transsexuals, transvestites, trans-everything! Gay couples who wanted to adopt, gay men hounded by the press, and a few out-and-out 'good-time girls'. Everyone was very chatty because of 'telly nerves', so we had a chance to talk about Jesus and faith to people from totally different lifestyles. After all, when was the last time you saw a bloke walk into your church dressed as Little Bo-Peep and ask you what you believe in? Exactly! (But what a great chance to talk about the parable of the Lost Sheep...)

The thing about TV is that you think of witty things to say a whole 10 minutes after they've cut to the commercials. In my case Nicky Campbell turned to me and said, 'Jon Bicknell, what would you say to this girl who's slept with hundreds of men?' What I meant to say was, 'Have you ever heard of the expression "playing hard to get?"' whereas what I actually said was, 'Has it ever been true love?' This was fine, I suppose, particularly as her sumo-wrestler-like boyfriend of the moment was sitting on the other side of the 'Condom Doctor' next to me (the Doc sends birthday cards from her surgery with condoms in them when her patients turn 14).

Joe did great, though, even with the dodgy haircut he was sporting at the time. And amazingly, in a brief moment of honesty, the glossy veneer of the equally glossy young blonde dropped. She ended up saying live on air that she wished she'd waited till she was married.

This amazed me, particularly as I was expecting her to say that sex makes life great, so the more sex, the greater the life. But in fact she was wistfully wishing to swap the whole lot for real love. She was actually on our side! As the programme ended, I asked another girl, who at 17 had slept with 47 men, if she thought she had a soul, and if so what she thought she was doing to it. Her answer also took me by surprise. The girl thought for a moment, then answered: 'Probably, and I'm probably destroying it.'

Afterwards, as people came up to Joe and thanked him, for a few brief moments it felt as if the whole 'You Must Have Sex Now' message was looking as vulnerable to collapse as a house of cards is to being blown over. We hadn't been slaughtered as I'd feared. No. Instead, like a featherweight boxer taking on a bigger opponent, we'd punched the darkness, and we'd made it bleed.

Since that first appearance, the requests for us to do this or that TV thing have kept on coming. Sounds dead showbiz, doesn't it! However, it's not just about us here doing all the chat, because what they want, what they really really want, are virgins! One woman researcher actually got a bit confused, and thought we were a commercial dating agency that guaranteed blind dates with virgins! We've decided to do some of the appearance requests, because it's such a powerful witness, but usually we've only used people we know personally. As tempting as it is to ask the members of True Love Waits when they write in if they want to be a 'TV celeb.', we've grown wary of the media, though not for the reasons that most people would imagine.

Some Christians imagine that the media go around on cloven hooves trying hard to hide the little pointy horns growing from their heads. However, Paul tells us in Ephesians 6:12 that the spiritual fight we're in isn't against flesh-and-blood people, but powers of darkness that are pulling the strings behind the scenes, and the media is no different from any other worldly business. But it is a business, and their business is making good television and finding out what makes people tick.

The vast majority of TV types we've come across so far have no strong desire to twist words, but they naturally want to find out how genuine people really are, and therefore they ask plenty of 'nitty-gritty' stuff long before you arrive in the TV studios, just to see how far they can go when the cameras are rolling.

It takes quite a lot out of anyone being questioned in front of an audience about very personal stuff. Usually, though, it's nowhere near as bad as you fear, and can even be great fun! Some people take to it like ducks to water. Fortunately we have people like Ed and Charli splashing about out there. Ed and Charli are long-time boy- and girlfriend, as well as strong believers (they're the two on the front cover). They are both now 17-year-olds, and were chosen to represent True Love Waits on a prime-time TV series about teenagers called *Teen Spirit*.

Incidentally, when Ed was 14, he was given a prophecy that he would be greatly used by God in evangelism. However, being followed around Amsterdam by a camera crew for several days' holiday isn't perhaps how he imagined it panning out – but why can't God use hi-tech too? It was also quite amusing to see them having to sign exclusive contracts to appear only for that particular TV production company. Real filmstar stuff!

For me personally, two other appearances stand

out. On *Esther*, an afternoon audience discussion programme, Jenny – a long-legged, attractive 21-year-old virgin – and I were invited along to give our point of view. We certainly made an impression – she for the right reasons, me probably for the wrong! Jenny came over so well that she couldn't have failed to impress anyone watching, and Esther Rantzen herself seemed totally for us. In fact, Jenny wasn't having any of it when another guest, Grub Smith, the sex 'expert' from *FHM* magazine, tried to show her the error of her ways. All he could end up doing was just recycling some corny chat-up lines, which actually made her look even better. That was Jenny.

I, on the other hand, got verbally slayed! The subject was one-night stands, and talking of grub, I decided I'd better point out to a serial one-night-stander that having over 100 blokes might just be a little bit of a grubby way to live. This opened the way for people to say I had no right to be so judgemental. And they did. Esther had actually wheeled in a Baptist minister to say it, but before he got there he'd already slipped up on that biblical banana skin: Saucy Solomon and his 300 mistresses…

You'll find King Solomon in the Old Testament, and to say that he liked the ladies would be an understatement. They made a famous film about him called *King Solomon's Mines*, which was about his spectacular wealth and his gold mines. It was not, as I once imagined, about him standing in front of a whole load of women saying, 'She's mine, she's mine, she's mine too...' The Bible says they (that's the women, not the mines) were the reason why his heart was turned away from God as he got older. I'm not surprised!

But leaving Solomon behind, it appeared obvious that it was now down to me to stick my neck out and end up looking like the intolerant, bigoted one – so I did! Only afterwards did something snappy come to mind: 'Lady, everybody's got a dark side, but yours is a black hole!' Nonetheless, complete strangers sidled up to me after the programme was broadcast to let me know that 'I would have said exactly the same thing!' – which helped. Oh well, some you lose...

...and some you win. It was Kilroy's morning show on BBC1, and it was a special moment. The discussion was about the age of consent, and sex generally. That time I did well with the snappy replies, but when

Kilroy sat down next to 'our' Jonny, another 20-year-old virgin (and voted 'Most Gorgeous Man' at last year's summer CYFA camp), his answer and its effect on the audience was so powerful, it even shocked Kilroy. Jonny said, 'Sex isn't the be-all and end-all it's made out to be. I'm 20, I'm a virgin, and I'm having a cracking life.' At this, the whole audience spontaneously applauded!

Bear in mind that this audience wasn't what you'd call 'holy' – in fact they were a right motley mix of types – but Jonny's words, combined with charm and intelligence, not to mention his boyish good looks (I didn't want to mention them, he made me!) stood out. So can you.

The best publicity for the True Love Waits message came about through an article published in *J–17* (the relaunched *Just 17* girls' magazine). They rang up and arranged to come down to photograph some of the youth group and get their quotes about True Love Waits. When the article entitled 'Would You Sign This Card?' came out in the September edition, they didn't bother to mention the address, because they thought it would just be a sort of 'and now we look at weird people and their weird ideas' type of article.

From the moment that edition was available, they were bowled over by girls phoning them wanting to know what address to write to. The response so impressed *J–17* that they had to put in a mini-addition to the article the following month.

From then on, we got bucket-loads of really inspiring letters. Every day, without fail, more arrived. It was truly fantastic to get each and every one of those letters, most from believers, but many from those who seemed to have little obvious faith. All were asking for a card, and many were very clear already why they felt it was important to wait. Letters are still sometimes arriving just as a result of that one magazine article.

This felt really exciting, and being able to write back and encourage them that they weren't on their own, and that other people did feel exactly the same way as they did, was the best of all. It was amazing how many of those letters started with: 'I think I'm the only person in my class/year/town who feels like this, but now I know others believe what I believe, I don't feel so alone with my views any more.'

One phone conversation in particular stood out for me. A girl who sounded very 'Essex' rang up and asked for the pack. When she told me her address, sure enough, her accent had already told me where in the country she came from! She guessed what I was thinking and added, 'I know what you're thinking about Essex girls, and you're right – all my mates are slappers, but I want to do True Love Waits.'

She then went on to tell me that the first time she slept with a bloke, he hadn't been happy with her 'performance', so he'd hit her in the face. Being drunk at the time, you could say that he never actually intended to hit her. Anyway, the outcome of that one session of passion was this: she gave him the gift of her virginity; he gave her the gift of a broken nose. Nice.

Which brings me neatly onto something to think about. Quite often when you go out, you aren't really sure whether it's love or what. Maybe you convince yourself that you're in love with the other person, or maybe it's the idea itself which so appeals, and you're actually in love with the idea of it, not the person. Maybe it feels absolutely genuine, and God really seems to have brought the two of you together. Maybe you desperately need someone who'll just be kind to you, and they were in the right place at the right time.

Whatever, just don't forget how fickle the heart is. This week you may be head-over-heels in love. You think it'll last forever. Next week, however, for no reason you can explain, your head's already wandering off, and the week after that your heels have done likewise. Last forever? Some people are proud of themselves if it lasts a fortnight! Check out the story of Jacob and Rachel in Genesis 29, and remember: if it's true love, which is a choice both of the head and of the heart, it really will be able to wait.

9

SeX aND POle-vAUltiNG

Pole-vaulting is a funny old sport. Have you ever wondered who thought of it, and why? You get a huge
great long poley thing, which looks like a piece of
scaffolding but is made by the same people who
manufacture elastic bands, then you run like a lunatic
and launch yourself, human-catapult-style, over a bar
miles up in the air. You then fall back down to earth
and land on a huge double bed. If you get it right you
leap about on the double bed (something my Mum

never let me do), but if you get it wrong you just lie there waiting for the bar to fall on you and smack you in the eye. Very bizarre.

Perhaps it started with people who'd locked themselves out of their houses and came home to find the windows to the bedroom fortunately left open. Then they spotted a handy pile of scaffolding poles from a neighbour's extension lying nearby ... and lo, it became a sport ... who knows?

If, however, like other Olympic sports, it's centuries old, then all they wanted to do in those days was jump into each other's castles. If that was the case, where does the double bed bit come into it? Somehow I can't see the castle owner lining up a nice, comfy bed for the incoming human catapult. A rusty old sharpened spike maybe, but that's not exactly sporting, is it?

One man who got this particular sport worked out is a bloke called Sergei Bubka. Back in 1988 he easily won the Olympic gold medal in Seoul, and then set world record after world record as the undisputed World Numero Uno. So naturally he became a 'bet-your-house-on-it' certainty for the gold medal at the

1992 Olympics in Barcelona. Unfortunately, if you did that, you'd now be homeless, because he won diddly-squat.

The reason he won nothing was completely his own fault. While all the other competitors were working their way up towards 17 feet, he'd decided he wasn't bothered with all that, and was nonchalantly finishing off his caviar and chips (or something). He'd decided, against his coach's advice, to do one huge vault at 18 feet, clean up and receive his gold medal without even breaking into a sweat. How wrong he proved to be. For some inexplicable reason his technique was out that fateful day, and because he'd chosen to set the mark of his first jump so high, there was no way he would even make the second round. He finished last, and he wasn't even Finnish. He was Russian. Rushin' to get out of there.

'What exactly has pole-vaulting got to do with sex?' I hear you ask. Well, both activities end up with you lying on your back on a bed thingy, but apart from that (and you smutty ones can stop that!), I'm going to tell you one of the lesser known parables, the Parable of the Pole-Vault. Like all good parables, and to use theological language, stuff is represented by things. In this case, sexy stuff (but not actually doing 'it') is represented by the bar. 'It' is represented by the big double bed thingy.

· Next, the pole is the gift of the Holy Spirit, and the competition represents the Christian life, surrounded by a stadium of well-wishers. And that's exactly what Hebrews 12:1 says. So now the question is, how high are you capable of jumping with this new-found power you've been given? There is one other part to mention: the part that Sergei took for granted.

Sergei imagined he was invincible, but he was up against a great opponent that day. The name of his opponent? It isn't shown in the record books, but it's this: Grav. E. Tee. While Sergei suffered, gravity got gold! Sergei didn't show gravity enough respect. If he had, perhaps he wouldn't have risked everything in the way he did, but either way he should never have taken it for granted.

No one disputes that, as a force, gravity is predictable. You know what it will do before it does it. Like Sergei and his fellow competitors, they could overcome it by vaulting high into the sky time after time after time, but they could never ignore it. So we're going to use gravity to represent human nature in our parable. You can never forget it, because you were born with it. It's a very useful force – most of the time – and most people have little hassle from it. But we Christians, we're the ones who were born to jump!

It's only when you try to jump, however, that you realize how strong its effect is. It's perhaps only when you've tried to jump that you've found yourself depressed at how powerful its hold over you seems to be. Maybe you've been frustrated with yourself when you feel sexy in a way that catches you off guard, particularly when you thought you'd got all that out of your system after praying about it.

Maybe you've been shocked when you're overwhelmed with a desire, a mix of curiosity and straightforward enjoyment, to watch an 18-certificate film, or when you find yourself flicking through a raunchy novel searching for the sexy bits. Or perhaps you've caught yourself on a hot summer's evening looking at your mate's boyfriend or girlfriend, and wondered how you can engineer things so you're the one alone with them at the next party. Yet you also know that if you do that, you'll lose the peace you feel inside. That's the Holy Spirit inside encouraging you to jump, but you'll also realize that gravity, your human nature, is wanting to keep you rooted to the spot.

It's time to jump if any of those thoughts, or their accompanying actions, fill you with a mixture of being appealed and being appalled. Like constantly fantasizing about someone in a way that dominates your thoughts. Or wanting to reach out and touch someone who's strictly out of bounds, or getting off with someone and it felt so wrong the next day. Or going so far that you didn't really want to stop anyway, and it was only because you knew her Mum might walk through the door that you stopped yourselves going all the way. Or masturbating like mad whilst dreaming about all of the above!

Whichever way, it's time to start. Maybe you have to live with some of these things, maybe you have to let go of some of these things, and maybe with some you just need to run! But what if you feel you're drowning in it? Well, I suggest for starters that you start! But don't set yourself a first jump that's too demanding. Sergei Bubka set himself too high a standard, and failed in a dramatic way. So what about you, what height are you going to set the bar? Those of you who read the Bible and rightly believe that it's a handbook for life still need to set the bar at a height you can manage.

I suggest that you set the bar somewhere between 'Be perfect, therefore, as your heavenly Father is perfect' (Matthew 5:48) and 'But I am only a worm and not a man!' (Psalm 22:6). The first is about a 25-footer – above what anyone has yet achieved, except Jesus. Don't set it there. After all, you'd never go out of the front door if you were trying to reach that standard and have utterly perfect thoughts all the time.

OK, shackle me down with heavy chains and call me guilty as charged, but why did Jesus bother saying those things if we could never actually make the jump? Well, it's like this. Firstly, when Jesus said this, he'd just taken a pop at the Pharisees for thinking they were already good enough in God's eyes. Now he turns on his own followers, who are feeling seriously smug because the religious lot are getting their noses put out of joint. But, with apologies for mixing my metaphors, Jesus now pulls the rug from under their noses too! Neither bunch can take the credit. God alone gets it.

But jump we Christians must. If you think, 'It doesn't really matter how I live now, because I've really, really tried to get near the height he's set it at, but it's just so high it's ridiculous. So now I'm going to stop trying, and admit defeat and forget it. Now I'm going to enjoy myself by jumping a few bones instead...' then you'd better look again. Start by reading Romans, chapters 5–8. Paul's argument is that he agrees, the bar is set way too high, far higher than we could possibly manage. But we're not just using our own legs to do the jumping. Now we've got help!

Paul writes that God's undeserved love is fully available for those who know they're weak-willed, worthless worms who set the bar at about two and a half feet, and still knock it off – i.e., you and me! He was actually writing it about himself too. Paul knew what it was like to fail a two-and-a-half-foot jump, and to stare up at the bar seemingly miles above his head and say, 'I'll never, ever be able to do that.' But Paul doesn't just shrug his shoulders and say, 'Oh well, human nature wins again,' because in those chapters he talks about two key things, two things with which God guarantees gold.

The first thing is that God isn't going to smack us over the head with the bar if we fail a titchy jump. In fact, the less we're able to jump, the more undeserved love God will bring to our aid. This undeserved love is what we call grace. Then the second thing is the Holy Spirit. He's the one to help us jump higher – because he's the pole. Father, Son and Poley Spirit!

Hands up those who've ever asked the question: 'As a Christian, how far can I go?' And you're not talking about a student travel pass, right? If the apostle Paul was your youth leader he would have started his talk by saying something like: 'Relax, however far you go is just fine, you're still covered by God's insurance policy [that "grace" stuff]. In fact, the further you go, the more you're covered, so you're OK.' Imagine that! Everyone would be grinning and winking at each other, and suddenly really looking forward to the next youth group social.

Then all of a sudden, like an aborigine's boomerang, his argument would come right round in an arc and be heading straight back again. He'd go on to say:

'But this isn't the question any of us want to ask any more, because it's not important to us any more, is it?'

'Yes it is!' would come an anguished voice from the back, followed by others taking their courage in both hands and joining in. St Paul would then say something like: 'But you're somebody! You've been chosen! You've been given something to help you leap higher off the ground than you could ever have imagined, and people will watch you and be amazed...'

And as he got more and more animated he would add: 'Sure, you can go straight to the lying on your back on the bed bit, but think about it ... the spectators out there are on your side. They're willing you to use that pole to vault over that bar, to see what you're capable of, to overcome gravity, to go for personal best, and once you've set your mark, and the bar's still up there as a testimony to how good you got, *then* you get to enjoy all the beddy stuff!'

In answer to the question, 'How far can I go?' some people have said, 'Don't play with it if you haven't got one!' which is fine – but what do you do about nipples? Answers on a postcard, please! Or maybe you take the fantastically woolly piece of advice given to one group of lads in a youth group: 'Don't touch a girl "upstairs"' (meaning her boobs, but the leader couldn't bring himself to say the word). Then he went on: 'And especially, lads, don't ever, ever touch a girl "downstairs"' (I don't need to tell you). Good, basic advice, but very unclear, because people had graphic images of being given permission to get naked and writhe around together, so long as you did it on the stairs.

Or you can take the view of many, some of whom would call themselves strong Christians, who can't bring themselves to stop short of anything except full penetrative sex. So they imagine everything else short of that is OK, which makes for an interesting list that includes passionate kissing; touching each other intimately both before and after undressing; undressing; lying down with each other semi or totally naked; mutual masturbation to orgasm using the hand, or using the tongue and the mouth for the same purpose – which is called oral sex, or more commonly, a blow job. The list is quite long.

So where do you draw the line? How far do you go? Is each and every one of those things on the list above, as some people say, 'the sign of my love for my partner'? One person said, 'How can it be wrong, when what we do only helps make us feel closer and more special with each other? After all, other sins that spring from hate and jealousy and bitterness are far more damaging than what we get up to, because ours are a natural expression of what we feel between ourselves, and we're never going to split up anyway, so it's got to be OK. Hasn't it...?'

This person went on, '...and isn't the Bible pretty vague in its advice anyway? And anyway they only talked about adultery in those days, and neither of us is married, and you have to be married before you can commit adultery, and anyway oral sex isn't mentioned in the Bible, so that's OK, and if God is a God of love he'll understand, and all I need to do is feel a bit sorry afterwards and I'm back on track ... and we do want to get married ... maybe ... and anyway...'

All of which is fine, perhaps. But remember there are two sides to every story, two sides on a coin, two coins in a fountain, two holes up a nose and two seats on a tandem. I don't want to make a dreary, depressing list of things that can go wrong, or mention people who are never really able to trust again because they've been so used and cynically abused, so I won't. I won't even mention pregnancy, unwanted babies, terminations, sexually transmitted diseases, AIDS, cervical cancer, or anything else along those lines. I won't, really I won't.

I won't even mention the horrible wrenching apart that happens if you've completely given yourself to someone, because surely it would be much easier if we all just had 'quickie' relationships of 'loving and leaving'? If we just went in for mutual transactions that hurt nobody, and nobody had any expectations of them going any further, wouldn't that be fine? Then we'd dispense with talk of love and faithfulness, because it's much too much like pushing water uphill, and public declarations of intent like marriage make it very much more difficult to engineer a painless withdrawal from any troublesome commitments, don't you agree...?

Huh! Good grief, I think I'd just drifted off in a weird, out-of-body experience! Where was I? Wherever it was, I think I need to say this one thing to bring me back. The Bible isn't 'pretty vague' about its advice. You just need to open your eyes.

If you recall the cracking film *A Few Good Men*, Kiefer Sutherland, as a US Marine Officer, was arguing in the courtroom with Tom Cruise that they could never have performed a 'Code Red' (a type of punishment on a wayward soldier) which resulted in the death of Private Santiago, because it wasn't in the Marine Manual. Tom Cruise then snatches up the Marine Manual and asks him to turn to the section where it mentions where the latrines (their toilets) are. Of course he can't, because, as Tom Cruise emphasizes, to find them you just follow where every other soldier is headed – or your nose!

Granted, if you want to find out what the Bible says specifically about sex you won't find it on too many pages. But please do look up the crystal-clear passages on the subject. Try that bit from Paul in 1 Corinthians 6:15–20. He writes the most dramatic words he uses anywhere, to point out that sex isn't just a physical joining where two people become one, it's also a powerful spiritual union where two people become one. You may not read about that in the papers, or see it in the films, but it's true, because when a Christian has sex with someone, it joins both your spirit and your body to that person. So, because Jesus has joined himself to you, and promised to stick his Holy Spirit to your human spirit, if my adding up is correct, that already means there are kind of three of you in the bed...

You can cover a budgie up in a cage if you don't want it to see something, or move it into another room, but Jesus is different. He promised he would never leave you, and because you can't separate your spirit from your body, he's also stuck with the person you're making love to. So you can't leave Jesus standing in the corner. He's joined to you, you're joined to him, and anyone else ... makes you think, doesn't it? It's not just the memory of what you do that sticks.

Equally importantly in that passage, Paul reminds us that we're stamped up 'Property of the King. Do Not Remove.' Now obviously, you can't see such a thing with the naked eye, and not many Christians I know would go in for the tattoo, but just like some special pens only show up under ultra-violet light, so this stamp is clearly visible to both angels and demons, and whatever else might be out there. We 'are not our own; we were bought at a price. Therefore honour God with your body' (1 Corinthians 6:20).

You simply have to follow the *flavour* of all the books to find out where the Bible goes on love and sex. It doesn't choose to emphasize it over and over again. Instead it's underpinned by the unity of male and female marriage and family that God went in for when he created us – the 'leaving and cleaving' principle of Genesis 2:24 that ministers always get mushy about in wedding services.

I was driven into by a van once, while I was just standing minding my own business and eating an ice-cream. Ice-cream everywhere – very nasty! I only needed to be driven into on one occasion before I learnt to stay away from reversing vans. It's the same with the Bible. Even the exotic and erotic book of the Song of Solomon in the Old Testament emphasizes one very clear thing: faithfulness, self-sacrifice and completeness are what sex with a uniquely special person *starts* from, not brings about.

Finally, then, for those of you with tidier minds than mine who are saying, 'That's all very well, but you haven't answered the question about how far I can go,' I tell you this: firstly, I'm known for never answering the question; secondly, supermarkets; and thirdly, I shan't anyway.

'Pardon?' I hear you ask. 'What's with supermarkets?' Well, anyone will tell you never to go to a supermarket on an empty stomach. Go shopping when you've eaten. Then you won't be tempted to get stupid things you don't want or need. The principle applies to sex too. Don't wait until the two of you are closing the spare bedroom door at someone's party, having been egged on by your mates, with a few beers under your belt, before you decide how far you'll go. Let's face it, at that moment, even vegetable quiche past its sell-by date starts looking delicious!

So that's supermarkets. Beyond that, however, I shan't advise you. Neither does the Bible specifically. It doesn't go in for the 'Don't remove each other's clothing and always keep one foot on the floor' type of advice, because you know some couples would still acrobatically manage to bonk fully dressed, thinking that meant they were still OK. No, the Saviour of the world talked about what came out of your heart as being the main issue, not what came out of an instruction book. Even if that wasn't the case, the question is still one that you'll have to answer alone. Without me.

Just you. And Jesus.

You, Jesus, and hopefully the one you love.

You, Jesus, the one you love, and the Christian friend you've pledged to be accountable to over the ins and outs of your love life.

Like I said, it's a serious decision you make alone...

...ish...

Sure, you can have a life that's a laugh, but also remember that you've been called to do heroic things with this, your one and only life. So go on, grab the pole and JUMP!